EIGHT DAYS THAT CHANGED THE WORLD

AN EASTER DEVOTIONAL

DR. JIM THOMAS

Eight Days That Changed The World: An Easter Devotional

ISBN 979-8-218-60877-4

EveryGen Press
Weatherford, Texas

Printed in the United States of America

Cover and Internal Art by Joseph Hutchinson and Jeff Carr

⊠EveryGen
P R E S S

Dedication

To the Congregation of North Side Baptist Church in Weatherford, Texas. May we always pursue our risen Savior and King and give our lives to "leading every generation toward a fully-formed life with Jesus."

CONTENTS

Acknowledgements

M uch assistance went into crafting this short devotional. Thank you to Lara Cook, Dr. Aaron Pardue, and Keith Warren for helping to edit each devotion. Thank you to Jeff Carr and Joseph Hutchinson for their creativity and artwork. Thank you to Jess Rainer and Craft Book Publishing for getting this book to publication in a very short amount of time. And thank you to you, the reader, for investing 8 weeks of your life in pursuing a deeper walk with Jesus through his passion week. May God richly bless you and grow you to be more like the one you profess and follow.

How to Use this Devotional

Eight Days That Changed The World is meant to take you on a journey from Palm Sunday to Easter Sunday over the eight weeks leading up to Easter. Each week is divided into six individual devotions from Monday through Saturday. Sunday's devotion is a simple Scripture meditation that introduces the next week. Each week corresponds to a day during Holy Week, or the final week of Jesus' earthly life. The goal is to help you pause, read, reflect, and pray through the most important week in human history. As you do, I believe that God will do a new work in you to remind, refresh, renew, and reignite a passion for the One who came, died, was buried, and rose again so that you might live. To God be the glory!

Introduction

There have been many events throughout history that have changed the course of the world. From the rise of ancient empires such as the Assyrians, Babylonians, Greeks, Romans, and Huns, to wars such as the Thirty Years War, the American Civil War, the Napoleonic War, and the World Wars of the 20th Century, these events still resonate in our minds and cultures today. Evolving technology has also worked to shape the world into who we are today. The invention of the printing press. The rise of the steam engine and the industrial age. The electrification of the world. The telegraph and telephone. The internal combustion engine. Digital technology such as the cell phone, the personal computer/tablet, and artificial intelligence. All of these have flattened the world and allowed us to understand, travel, and communicate on a level that was unprecedented in the past.

I could go on and on, but there was one event, made up of a series of related events that supersedes all other examples of transformation. Ironically, we don't see this event taking place in the great world capitals or among the great world powers, though one would play a role in the background. We don't see it happen among the powerful leaders of the world, though the one at its center would eventually be called "King of Kings and Lord of Lords." We don't see it happen through conquest or warmongering, but through a decided humility, suffering, and sacrifice. We don't see it in a temporary realignment of borders or nationalities, but in an eternal realignment of the lives of anyone who will receive its outcome and promises. We see it happen over the course of 8 Days, and these Eight Days That Changed The World.

Jim Thomas, Ph.D.
Weatherford, Texas
January 2025

First Sunday of Holy Week

When they approached Jerusalem, at Bethphage and Bethany near the Mount of Olives, he sent two of his disciples and told them, "Go into the village ahead of you. As soon as you enter it, you will find a colt tied there, on which no one has ever sat. Untie it and bring it. If anyone says to you, 'Why are you doing this?' say, 'The Lord needs it and will send it back here right away.'" So they went and found a colt outside in the street, tied by a door. They untied it, **5** and some of those standing there said to them, "What are you doing, untying the colt?" **6** They answered them just as Jesus had said; so they let them go. They brought the colt to Jesus and threw their clothes on it, and he sat on it. Many people spread their clothes on the road, and others spread leafy branches cut from the fields. Those who went ahead and those who followed shouted:

> ***Hosanna!***
> **Blessed is he who comes**
> **in the name of the Lord!**
> Blessed is the coming kingdom
> of our father David!
> ***Hosanna*** in the highest heaven!

He went into Jerusalem and into the temple. After looking around at everything, since it was already late, he went out to Bethany with the Twelve.

- Mark 11:1-11 (CSB)

Monday

Scripture

When they approached Jerusalem, at Bethphage and Bethany near the Mount of Olives, he sent two of his disciples and told them, "Go into the village ahead of you. As soon as you enter it, you will find a colt tied there, on which no one has ever sat. Untie it and bring it. If anyone says to you, "Why are you doing this?" say, "The Lord needs it and will send it back here right away." - Mark 11:1-2 (CSB)

Reflection

Have you ever had to do something where you didn't know the outcome was sure? The disciples lived in that world. Think about it. Jesus asked them to do some strange stuff. Come to me on the water... Bring me those loaves and fish... Collect all the leftovers... Bring that blind beggar to me... Don't keep the children from me... Go out two by two and do what I have been doing...

Strange stuff. But each time, as they trusted in him, the outcome was nothing short of miraculous. Of course, when they took their eyes off him (cue Peter walking on water), things didn't go so well.

On the first Sunday of Holy Week, Jesus gives another strange command. Two undisclosed disciples are to go into a local village and borrow someone else's colt, the foal of a donkey. Talk about nerve wracking. We don't know what these two were thinking that day, and we know that they ended up obeying Jesus, but could some questions have been bouncing around in their minds? What if the colt isn't there? What if the owners put up a fight? What if we are arrested? What if... What if...

Sounds vaguely familiar, doesn't it? Echoing back to the Garden of Eden, we have all made our excuses, internally or externally, for why we shouldn't obey God. The woman you gave me... (Adam), the serpent deceived me... (Eve), who should I say sent me, I'm not very eloquent in speech... (Moses), I won't believe until I touch his hands and side... (Thomas). We have all made our excuses. *But excuses excuse us from being in the center of God's will and being a part of something much bigger than ourselves.* What has God called you to do? What excuses have you made? Will you step out in faith today and simply obey Him? The outcome might be miraculous.

PRAYER

Father, help me to walk by faith. It is so easy for me to only take steps in obedience to you when I can see the path. But I know that many times you will ask me to do things that don't make sense in the moment or that push against my self-will. During those times, teach me to listen, to trust, and to step out in obedience to your word and will. Give me courage to walk where I haven't walked yet. In Jesus' name. Amen.

NOTES:

TUESDAY

SCRIPTURE

> So those who were sent left and found it just as he had told them.
> As they were untying the colt, its owners said to them, "Why
> are you untying the colt?" "The Lord needs it," they said. - Luke
> 19:32-34 (CSB)

REFLECTION

Obedience is hard. We have all struggled with it. From childhood
we have this sense of a dependent independence, where we want
the safety and security of parents, home, and family, but want to
do things our way. We see it in infants that throw tantrums or
food across the room. We see it in the "dead drop" of toddlers in
department stores, where they simply go limp and stop moving
when they don't want to do what their parents ask of them. We
see it in pre-teen and teenage attitudes and rebellious behavior.
And we see it in the immature or addictive behavior of adults who
have not given up "childish things" (1 Corinthians 13:11).

But the Gospels and the New Testament speak to the intentional correlation of faith and obedience. Peter challenges his
readers by saying, "As obedient children, do not be conformed to
the desires of your former ignorance. But as the one who called
you is holy, you also are to be holy in all your conduct; for it is
written, Be holy, because I am holy" (1 Peter 1:14-16). John says,
"For this is what love for God is: to keep his commands. And his

commands are not a burden, because everyone who has been born of God conquers the world. This is the victory that has conquered the world: our faith" (1 John 5:3-4). Jesus is even more direct when he says, "If you love me, you will keep my commands... If anyone loves me, he will keep my word. My Father will love him, and we will come to him and make our home with him. The one who doesn't love me will not keep my words. The word that you hear is not mine but is from the Father who sent me" (John 14:15, 23-24).

After Jesus' instructions for the disciples to go and find the colt in a nearby village, they respond by faith and go. When they arrive, both Luke and Mark say that they find it just as Jesus had said. *So, faith is now activated in obedience.* They untie the colt and prepare to return to Jesus, but then their possible fears are realized. The owners walk up, confront them, and ask why they are taking the colt. The disciples, now boldened by the reality of their faith in action, respond as Jesus had instructed. As such, the owners respond by letting them take the foal (Mark 11:6).

What is the last thing Jesus asked you to do? Maybe it was something you read in Scripture that you know needs to be applied to your life. Maybe it was a prompting of the Holy Spirit toward a certain word to be spoken or an action to be taken. Did you obey? What was the outcome? Was there resistance, road-blocks, or persecution? Did you remain faithful? What was the outcome of your obedience? Where did you see God working? A seminary professor once said, "The basic pattern in Scripture is *always* faith, leading to obedience, *resulting* in blessing." How will you obey today?

PRAYER

Father, help me to know your will today. As you reveal it to me, help me to take intentional and direct steps of obedience as I follow the leading of your Spirit. Please give me courage and resolve to do what you have asked me to do. I will do it all for your glory. In Jesus' name. Amen.

NOTES:

Wednesday

Scripture

They brought the colt to Jesus and threw their clothes on it, and he sat on it. - Mark 11:7 (CSB)

Reflection

Have you ever been a part of something bigger than yourself? Maybe it was a sporting event, a concert, or an academic or vocational endeavor, but you found yourself a player in a bigger story. You realized your efforts helped to supplement a greater effort. When we realize this, we can respond in two ways. We can become arrogant and prideful, thinking we should be the center of attention and praise. Or we can realize our contribution is valuable, but is limited by our own knowledge, foresight, and ability. It is only when our contribution is added to that of others that something bigger emerges, and the outcome isn't as much about us as it is about something greater.

The scene on Sunday now switches from the disciples' obedience to Jesus' obedience. Jesus had always been obedient to his Father's will. From the earliest age Jesus said to his earthly parents, "Didn't you know that it was necessary for me to be in my Father's house?" (Luk 2:49). During his public ministry, he would remind his disciples of his resolute obedience to his Father. He told them, "I can do nothing on my own. I judge only as I hear, and my judgment is just, because I do not seek my own will, but the will of him who sent me" (John 5:30). Regarding his words and preaching, he said, "For I have not spoken on my own, but the Father himself who sent me has given me a command to say everything I have said" (John 12:49). He then summarizes his purpose in obedience to the Father by saying, "...so that the world may know that I love the Father, I do as the Father commanded me" (John 14:31).

Now, on the first Sunday of Holy Week, we see that obedience lived out one more time as he mounts the colt. This action, which might mean little to us today, and might seem a little bizarre, was significant in the life and hope of Israel. Over 500 years before, the prophet Zechariah prophesied that the coming Messiah would ride on a donkey's foal. He said, *"Rejoice greatly, Daughter Zion! Shout in triumph, Daughter Jerusalem! Look, your King is coming to you; he is righteous and victorious, humble and riding on a donkey, on a colt, the foal of a donkey"* (Zech. 9:9; Matt. 21:4,5). Though for the most part, Jesus had kept His identity a secret except to those closest to Him, He now unequivocally announces who He proclaims to be: The Coming Messiah! Riding in on a foal reveals two things about Jesus. First, He identifies with the line of David as the donkey was seen as a royal animal in David's day. Second, He is *"humble and riding on a donkey,"* which typifies Jesus' entire ministry, as a servant of God who was not unwilling to set aside His status as God to serve and save mankind (Philippians 2:5-11).

How are you helping in Jesus' mission to redeem the world? Maybe your part seems minuscule and insignificant, similar to retrieving a colt or placing blankets on it. But as we act in obedience to Jesus' call on our lives, we participate in the larger work of God in the world. How will you do so today?

PRAYER

Father, thank you for your invitation to join you in your mission to the world. Thank you for the personality, talents, gifts, passions, and life experience that you have given me so that I might do as you instruct me. Help me to do just that today. No matter how insignificant it might seem, help me to follow you and obey you as you do your work to draw all people to yourself. In Jesus' name. Amen.

NOTES:

Thursday

Scripture

Many people spread their clothes on the road, and others spread leafy branches cut from the fields. Those who went ahead and those who followed shouted: *Hosanna!* Blessed is he who comes in the name of the Lord! Blessed is the coming kingdom of our father David! *Hosanna* in the highest heaven! - Mark 11:8-10 (CSB)

Reflection

We are all worshippers. The question is, "What is the object of your worship?" Pastor Louie Giglio defines worship as "*our response to what we value most.*" So, take a quick evaluation today. What do you value most? No, really, write those things down. Here, I will give you some space to do it.

_____

_____

_____

Now, how many of those things fall short of being true objects of worship? I have always seen worship as the result of our intentionally placed attention (mind) and affection (heart) on what we truly desire and treasure. One of my favorite Old Testament verses is Jonah 2:8. The prophet says, "Those who cling to worthless idols forfeit the grace that could be theirs" (NIV,1984). An idol is anything or anyone we think deserves our affection and attention other than God. But we tend to cling to those things, don't we? We have a propensity to hold on to them like our lives depend on them. But in the end, anything less than God will fail us. Things are not built to save, sustain, or fully satisfy.

So, Jesus' entry into Jerusalem is the proclamation that one has come who can save, sustain, and fully satisfy. And the crowd senses that something bigger is happening. This was not just a famous, itinerate rabbi coming to the big city at Passover. He was not just the next mega-church preacher, holding a rally in the local stadium. This was something more. This was salvation riding on a donkey! As we saw yesterday, the donkey symbolized the coming of the Messiah. Now the people lay clothes and palm branches, a symbol of nationalistic unity, before him, not unlike we would roll out a red carpet for a dignitary today. They then shout, "Hosanna." The word Hosanna means "save" or "save us." It is a cry of desperation. It is a cry of invitation. It is a cry that leads to worship as they proclaim, "Blessed is he who comes in the name of the Lord! Blessed is the coming kingdom of our father David!" For the King has come.

As you evaluate the objects of worship in your life, what idols need to be torn down? Maybe it is pride, selfishness, or greed. Maybe it is a certain thing, like money, possessions, or position. Or maybe it is a certain person or people in your life? Regardless, will you lay them down before the feet of Jesus so that you won't forfeit the grace that could be yours?

PRAYER

Father, I confess to you today that I have a great tendency toward idolatry. I put feelings, things, and/or people as the priority in my life instead of you. Today, I lay those things down at your feet. I invite you to rule as the King of my life, as the only One who is worthy of my attention and affection. So, today, I cry out "*Hosanna!* Blessed is he who comes in the name of the Lord! Blessed is the coming kingdom of our father David! *Hosanna* in the highest heaven!" In Jesus' name. Amen.

NOTES:

Friday

Scripture

His disciples did not understand these things at first. However, when Jesus was glorified, then they remembered that these things had been written about him and that they had done these things to him. - John 12:16 (CSB)

Some of the Pharisees from the crowd told him, "Teacher, rebuke your disciples."- Luke 19:39 (CSB)

Then the Pharisees said to one another, "You see? You've accomplished nothing. Look, the world has gone after him!"- John 12:19 (CSB)

Reflection

Misunderstandings are a part of life. We have all been there. We have said one thing, and people heard something different, even opposite of what was intended. Maybe the cause was that we didn't communicate it clearly, use the appropriate language to convey what we wanted to say, or didn't speak with the right inflection of voice so that the wrong emotion was delivered. Or maybe, they, as we do many times, were thinking ahead of what we were saying, drawing conclusions before we even finished speaking. Regardless, misunderstandings are common, but they can lead us into more dangerous territory if we are not careful, like opposition or even persecution.

Jesus was no stranger to misunderstandings, opposition, and persecution. We see it all throughout his public ministry. The crowds, disciples, and religious leaders constantly misunderstood his teachings, especially when he taught in parables. Once his teachings and miracles became more controversial, such as elevating himself as the same as the Father (John 10:30) and healing on the sabbath, the religious leaders began to push back and the crowds followed suit, even trying to throw him off a cliff (Luke 4:29-30) or stone him (John 8:59). Regardless, Jesus was resolute in his faithfulness and obedience to his Father.

At the end of that first Sunday of Holy Week, we see several groups represented, the disciples, the pharisees, and as we will see tomorrow, the crowds. Each fell into the categories of misunderstanding, oppression, and/or persecution. John reveals that his disciples didn't understand the Triumphal Entry. They were living in the moment, reveling in the praise of the crowd and the euphoria of the moment, without seeing the larger meaning behind it all. (Until later.) The Pharisees pushed back against this blatant display of Messianic demonstration. They pushed back against Jesus, telling him to settle down the elaborate exuberance of his disciples. They also saw that their efforts over the years to extinguish this movement were failing and that drastic measures might have to be taken soon.

When was the last time you were misunderstood? How did you respond or try to correct the misunderstanding? When have you been oppressed or persecuted because of your faith in Jesus? How did you respond? How will you the next time it happens?

Paul reminds us, "...all who want to live a godly life in Christ Jesus will be persecuted" (2 Timothy 3:12).

PRAYER

Father, if I am honest, I hate being misunderstood. I want people to hear me clearly and know my heart. But I know that misunderstandings will happen. It is good to know that I am in good company because you were misunderstood as well. Help me to respond as you do, with patience, grace, and mercy. Help me also to know that if I live for you that oppression and persecution will come. When it does, may I not "be surprised when the fiery ordeal comes among you to test you, as if something unusual were happening to you. Instead, rejoice as you share in the sufferings of Christ, so that you may also rejoice with great joy when his glory is revealed" (1 Peter 4:12). In Jesus' name. Amen.

NOTES:

Saturday

Scripture

When he entered Jerusalem, the whole city was in an uproar, saying, "Who is this?" The crowds were saying, "This is the prophet Jesus from Nazareth in Galilee."- Matthew 21:10-11 (CSB)

Meanwhile, the crowd, which had been with him when he called Lazarus out of the tomb and raised him from the dead, continued to testify. This is also why the crowd met him, because they heard he had done this sign. - John 12:17-18 (CSB)

Reflection

If you have ever been in a leadership position, you know this truth: the crowd is fickle. One day they like you, and the next, not so much. The reasons are varied. It could be the result of one or a series of poor leadership decisions, a threat to the personal preferences of the crowd or the threat of organizational change, a lack of performance by one or the other, or it could be a relational riff between leaders and the crowd. We see this in many areas of life. If our sports team doesn't perform, we may still be on board as a fan, but our ecstasy from their last championship now turns to criticism and vitriol at their current failure. If a politician has campaigned for and has been elected based on his or her promises of a better life for their constituents and then doesn't deliver, those followers might quickly move on to another candidate.

Jesus was not immune to the fickleness of crowds. They had gathered around him from the beginning of his public ministry. Some members of those crowds were genuine, but others were simply there for the show or for their own benefit. As author and speaker Bill Hull says, "The crowd surrounding Jesus was interested in him. But they were primarily interested in what Jesus could do for them. He was a means to an end."* We will see this lived out in greater detail as we progress through Holy Week, but for now the crowds were jubilant.

Jesus seemed to cause a stir wherever he went, from the shores of the Sea of Galilee to the Temple Courts, his presence, teaching, and miraculous works attracted crowds and enacted a sort of religious frenzy around him for a season. Of course, we see the fickleness of the crowds even in the early part of Jesus ministry. In John 6, in one of the great "I am" statements, Jesus had said that he was the "bread of life" (John 6:35). As such, he invites the people to eat of his flesh and drink of his blood. Of course, Jesus was not being literal, but was pointing forward to his death and the price that He would pay for all mankind. The "eating" then was symbolic of placing faith in Jesus' sacrificial atonement for people, not a literal eating and drinking. Such an idea would be pagan in nature, as the pagan cults of the day would eat raw meat and drink blood, which was strictly forbidden for the Jews. The crowd admits this is a hard saying and John says, ironically in John 6:66, "From that moment many of his disciples turned back and no longer accompanied him." But now, on the end of

---

* Bill Hull, *Conversion and Discipleship: You Can't Have One Without The Other* (Zondervan, 2016), 60.

the first Sunday, the crowd asked in excitement, "Who is this?" and testified to his miraculous power in his most recent miracle of raising Lazarus from the dead.

How easily are you swayed by the voice of the crowd? Is your faith in Jesus based on him or on what he can do for you and those around you? How can you remain faithful when those around you aren't?

PRAYER

Father, help me to listen to your voice and strive to only obey you. For you are my good shepherd and I want to follow where you lead. Please help me when I am swayed either by the praise or the criticism of the crowd. Help me to find your voice amid the noise. When I do, lead me to green pastures and help me to be faithful to you. In Jesus' name. Amen.

NOTES:

MONDAY OF HOLY WEEK

They came to Jerusalem, and he went into the temple and began to throw out those buying and selling. He overturned the tables of the money changers and the chairs of those selling doves, and would not permit anyone to carry goods through the temple. He was teaching them: "Is it not written, My house will be called a house of prayer for all nations? But you have made it a den of thieves!" The chief priests and the scribes heard it and started looking for a way to kill him. For they were afraid of him, because the whole crowd was astonished by his teaching. Whenever evening came, they would go out of the city.

- Mark 11:15-19 (CSB)

Monday

Scripture

> The next day when they went out from Bethany, he was hungry. Seeing in the distance a fig tree with leaves, he went to find out if there was anything on it. When he came to it, he found nothing but leaves; for it was not the season for figs. He said to it, "May no one ever eat fruit from you again!" And his disciples heard it. - Mark 11:12-14 (CSB)

Reflection

I hate it when I get hangry! You read that correctly, not just hungry, but hangry. Have you ever been there? The dictionary definition of hangry, and yes it does exist as a real word, is to be "irritable or angry because of hunger." Maybe you miss a meal, like breakfast, and the day keeps dragging on with appointments, responsibilities, or busy work that must get done. The idea of eating just escapes your mind. Until you sense your attitude changing. You start to get snippy with co-workers, classmates, or family members. Your patience in what you are trying to accomplish starts to diminish. You wonder why you are getting so emotional. And then you remember: you haven't eaten.

Jesus got hungry too. He was fully God, yes, but also fully human, and as such we see him get hungry. That is the case in Mark 11 as he and his disciples make their way to the Temple on the Monday morning of Holy Week. The absence of figs elicits a response from Jesus. In fact, he ends up cursing the tree so that it won't produce fruit again. But before we begin to think that Jesus' emotions were out of control, we need to see the bigger picture of what is going on here. In fact, Jesus was very much in control of his emotions here, even though hungry.

The Temple plays a central role in the final week of Jesus' life. In fact, it is a key idea in Christianity that Jesus acts as the ultimate Temple, the dwelling place of God and man. The fig tree, then, becomes illustrative of the spiritual barrenness of the second Temple in Jerusalem and its leaders as Mark demonstrates by saying that it was not the season for figs (vs. 13b). The disciples overhear Jesus' cursing of the tree and are perplexed. What has this tree done? Well, nothing. Jesus is being prophetic. He is illustrating the future of the Temple in Jerusalem. Because it hasn't produced spiritual fruit for God's glory, it will be destroyed. Of course, the Temple would be destroyed by the Romans in 70 A.D. fulfilling Jesus' earlier prophecy during Holy Week.

This begs a huge question in our lives: are we bearing fruit for the Kingdom of God? The New Testament speaks of several kind of "fruit": the fruit of character (Fruit of the Spirit), the fruit of good works, the fruit of evangelism, the fruit of prayer, and the fruit of praise. All this fruit should typify a believer's life and walk. In other words, each expression of Fruit that we encounter in the Scripture demonstrates what a Christian should look like.

As such, a life outside of Christ is a fruitless life. But a life lived by abiding in Jesus will bear much fruit. Jesus disciples then ask him about the fig tree. Jesus responds by demonstrating this kind of fruit. He says, "Have faith in God. Truly I tell you, if anyone says to this mountain, 'Be lifted up and thrown into the sea,' and does not doubt in his heart, but believes that what he says will happen, it will be done for him. Therefore I tell you, everything you pray and ask for—believe that you have received it and it will be yours. And whenever you stand praying, if you have anything against anyone, forgive him, so that your Father in heaven will also forgive you your wrongdoing" (Mark 11:22-25). This can only happen when we live or abide in Jesus. In fact, in John's gospel, he says, "I am the true vine, and my Father is the gardener. Every branch in me that does not produce fruit he removes, and he prunes every branch that produces fruit so that it will produce more fruit. You are already clean because of the word I have spoken to you. Remain in me, and I in you. Just as a branch is unable to produce fruit by itself unless it remains on the vine, neither can you unless you remain in me. I am the vine; you are the branches. The one who remains in me and I in him produces much fruit, because you can do nothing without me" (John 15:1-5).

PRAYER

Father, help me to bear fruit for your glory and your Kingdom. I confess that in the past I have failed in this endeavor. It is only by your Holy Spirit that I can be who you have called me to be and do what you have called me to do. So, please bear fruit through me as you form the character of Christ in me and as you give me the courage and boldness to share the gospel with others. I want to be consistently connected to you, the vine, so please forgive me when I have strayed. I don't want to look like the fig tree, so if you need to prune me so that I might grow again, please cut me back. Make me who you are calling me to be. In Jesus' name. Amen.

NOTES:

TUESDAY

SCRIPTURE

Jesus went into the temple and threw out all those buying and selling. - Matthew 21:12a (CSB)

REFLECTION

We all have expectations when we go to church. We expect there to be parking in our preferred lot. We expect to be greeted at the doors and find a hospitable environment on Sundays. We expect to see our friends in small groups or in worship. We expect a dynamic worship service with a message that is biblical and applicable to our lives. We expect the coffee to be made, donuts or other breakfast food to be available, and our kids and student areas to be teeming with life. But there are times when our expectations are not met. People aren't as friendly as they should be, the worship service lacked in vitality, our small group lesson didn't seem to address the current issues in our life, and the kids should have simply stayed in bed this morning!

The Temple was the dwelling place of God with man. It was a place of holiness, reverence, sacrifice, and worship. But over the course of the 400 years between Malachi and Matthew, it had become something different. Though the Jews still revered the Temple mount, it had become a place of "dead orthodoxy," a place where religious practice took place, but love for and devotion to God had waned. As a result, convictions and practices had been compromised and their original intent had been supplanted with questionable and even nefarious means.

Though it wasn't the first time Jesus had seen such goings on in the Temple courts, now, in the final week of his life, he responds. In fact, many scholars believe this could have been his second response to such activity, the first coming at the beginning of his ministry as recorded in John 2:13-22. So, he enters and drives out those buying and selling. As pilgrims travelled from distant lands to celebrate the Passover, it would be highly unlikely that they would bring animals that were approved for sacrifice. As a convenience and necessity, merchants would set up shop to provide for their needs. That would not be a problem, but they had set up shop in the Court of the Gentiles and not outside the Temple courts, which was inappropriate, along with charging exorbitant prices, and so taking advantage of those coming to worship. Therefore, Jesus responds by driving out the merchants.

What are your expectations when you go to church? Are you more concerned about your comfort or about God's glory? Are you more concerned about how programs will be run than having a right heart before the Lord? Our first expectation should be to meet with and worship God with His people. We should also go with an expectation that God will move among us, drawing people to Himself and sending us out to live lives in holiness and obedience. If our goals are anything else, we must correct them and turn our worship back to God.

PRAYER

Father, show me your expectations when I come to worship you. Whether it is privately in my own house or corporately in your house, give me "clean hands and a pure heart" (Psalm 24:4) when I come before you and as I live my life before you every day. Help me to come to church each week expectant: hoping and waiting on you to do a work in my life and in the life of others around me. Make me sensitive to their needs and how you might use me in their lives as well. Thank you for the privilege of knowing and worshipping you. May I never take that for granted. In Jesus' name. Amen.

NOTES:

WEDNESDAY

SCRIPTURE

He overturned the tables of the money changers and the chairs of those selling doves. He said to them, "It is written, my house will be called a house of prayer, but you are making it a den of thieves!"- Matthew 21:12b-13 (CSB)

REFLECTION

After the opening remarks in verse 12:21a, Matthew then tells us exactly who Jesus drove out and why. He turned over the tables of the money changers, drove out those selling sacrificial doves, and reminded the people of the true purpose of the Temple, that it was to be a house of prayer for all nations (Mark 11:17). By turning it into a place of commerce, the religious leaders had made it a "den of thieves," a place where unscrupulous dealings were being conducted. But Jesus reminds them that prayer and the worship of God are primary in their relationship with Him.

Prayer is a foundation of our walk with Christ. Through Christ, the doors of Heaven have been opened wide, and we now have access to God through Jesus. As a result, we can pray, lifting our petitions, supplications, praise, and requests to Him in any place at any time. Pastor and author Eugene Peterson aptly describes prayer as "answering God." Why would he say that? Well, because all we know about God is due to the revelation of himself to his creation. Without that revealing, we wouldn't know who he is or how we can know and respond to him. So, prayer, then, becomes our answer to God's revelation. In fact, Jesus even gave us a model so that we would know how to pray. In Matthew 6:9-13, he says, "Therefore, you should pray like this:

Our Father in heaven,
your name be honored as holy.
Your kingdom come.
Your will be done
on earth as it is in heaven.
Give us today our daily bread.
And forgive us our debts,
as we also have forgiven our debtors.
And do not bring us into temptation,
but deliver us from the evil one
For yours is the kingdom and the power and the glory forever. Amen."

PRAYER

Pray the Lord's Prayer from Matthew 6 this morning. Insert any specific praise, petition, or supplication that you want as you pray through it.

NOTES:

Thursday

Scripture

The blind and the lame came to him in the temple, and he healed them. - Matthew 21:14 (CSB)

Reflection

There have been several questions that have been asked of me or those around me that have changed my life. One such question was asked at a Deacon's Retreat. Dr. Richard Blackaby had come in as our guest speaker and was teaching our deacons about spiritual leadership. During that teaching he asked a question that not only changed my life but my ministry. He simply asked, "Where have you seen God working around you this week?"

It seems like a simple question until you start to think about it. In fact, it raises more. Is God working around me? Am I watching to see where God is at work around me, in my family, at my work or school, in my community? Am I walking with him faithfully enough to know if it is him? If I have noticed him working, how have I responded? Was I obedient to his invitation to join him in his work? Did someone miss out on a blessing because I was clueless to the work of God? Did I?

It is amazing, though it shouldn't be, that once we are on the same page with God, abiding in him, listening to him, obeying him, and honoring him in our worship, he reveals his purposes and invites us to join him in his mission to make all things new. But when we are too busy with our own agendas, our own self-gratification or self-glorification, or focused on our own comfort or pleasure, we aren't even able to see the needs right in front of us.

When was the last time you saw God working around you? How did you respond? Did you have eyes to see, ears to hear, and a heart to understand? Will you look for his activity and invitation today?

PRAYER

Father, there are so many needs in the world. It can get so overwhelming, and my contribution can seem insignificant. But I realize today that you are inviting me into your work, into your compassion, into your love, and into your work of reconciliation. Please help me to see you working around me today. Help me to abide in you, listen to you, and obey you as you call me to serve you and others. Help me truly see "Your kingdom come. Your will be done on earth as it is in heaven" today. In Jesus' name. Amen.

NOTES:

Friday

Scripture

The chief priests and the scribes heard it and started looking for a way to kill him. For they were afraid of him, because the whole crowd was astonished by his teaching. - Mark 11:18 (CSB)

Reflection

There are several temptations that can destroy character: pride, wrath, gluttony, lust, sloth, and greed. Six of the seven deadly sins mentioned in Scripture, are key culprits in the destruction of the soul. But one other ranks right up there as well, and that is jealousy. The green-eyed monster known as jealousy has gotten the best of all of us. At some point we have said, "Look at how beautiful/handsome they are. I wish I looked like that." "See the power/ position they have. Boy, if only I had that kind of power/ position, what I could do…," "If only I had their salary…," "If only my kids were like theirs…," "If I only had that talent…," and on and on. We are all victims of jealousy and its after-effects, judgmental-ism, bitterness, and even worse.

The religious leaders, well most of them, but not all, felt the sting of jealousy regarding Jesus. Not only did they not agree with much of his theology or proclamations regarding them, but were put off by his insinuation that he was the Messiah and that his Father was God. After his outburst in the Temple and healing of those who came to him, they had finally had enough. Their jealousy turned to rage, and their rage turned to plots of violence. All of this was driven by fear. The crowds were streaming to him, they were astonished by his teaching, and worst of all, they were on the verge of worshiping him! Would the religious leaders lose their power and influence over the people? Would Jesus rise-up and supplant them? Would the people be led astray by another would-be Messianic figure, for there had been many. Would the Romans crack down on them if Jesus was proclaimed by the people to be the King of the Jews? So much fear.

How has jealousy hindered your capacity to see Jesus for who he is? Who or what has become an idol in your life keeping you from being astonished by Jesus and worshiping him as your Savior and Lord? What needs to change regarding the green-eyed monster?

PRAYER

Father, I confess to you today that I have struggled with jealousy. I also admit that I can't defeat this monster on my own. So, today I give you my jealousy regarding _____. I know that you are the giver of all good things and that you work all things for the good of those who love you. Therefore, I repent of holding onto those feelings of insecurity and envy. I surrender them to you and ask that you become the priority of my life, the holder of my identity, and the provider for my needs. Thank you for loving me that much. In Jesus' name. Amen.

NOTES:

Saturday

Scripture

Whenever evening came, they would go out of the city. - Mark 11:19 (CSB)

Reflection

I love naps! Some people can't nap. They either just can't sleep during the day or feel like it would ruin their night's rest if they took a nap. But I love naps! In fact, napping was an unofficial class I would take each semester during the afternoon in college. I would wake up rested and ready to do homework or go out with my friends (which I probably did more). I still nap, when appropriate, and it is a source of physical renewal for me. But as I have gotten older, I have realized that I need more than just physical renewal. I need rest and renewal in every aspect of my life. I need mental renewal, emotional renewal, and spiritual renewal. And so do we all. So, here is a question for you today? What renews you? I think there are probably some commonalities among people, but for most of us the answer will be different. Regardless, we need to find those things that help breathe new life and joy into us. We need to find those times that set us up for the next season of life. We need to find those places that will help renew us so that we can navigate the inevitable crises we will face. We need to learn to rest so that we might be the best we can be for God and others.

There is a healthy theology of rest in Scripture. We see it from the beginning when God rested after six days of creation (though he didn't need the rest, his rest served as an example for his creation). We see prophets, priests, and kings take appropriate times to rest so that they might serve God better. Even Jesus would withdraw throughout his earthly ministry for times of rest and renewal with either his disciples or his Father.

If all these saints, and God himself rested, then how much more should we? There is no command in Scripture to burn out! Today, will you find some time to rest? Maybe it's just for 15, 20, or 30 minutes, but find a place of respite and reconnect with God, the giver and sustainer of life. Get away from the hustle and bustle and breathe again. Breathe in. Then breathe out. Then breath in. Then breathe out. Keep it going. Rest.

PRAYER

Father, I confess to you today that sometimes I don't rest well. I can allow the worries, stresses, and circumstances of my life to ball me up into a knot of anxiety, worry, restlessness, and exhaustion. Please help me to find the physical, mental, emotional, and spiritual space that I need in your presence to be refreshed and renewed. Use that time and space to do a new work in me so that I might be more usable for you and to those around me. Help me to breathe again. Thank you for the life you breathe into me. In Jesus' name. Amen.

NOTES:

TUESDAY OF HOLY WEEK

Now Jesus began to go all over Galilee, teaching in their synagogues, preaching the good news of the kingdom, and healing every disease and sickness among the people.

- Mathew 4:23 (CSB)

Monday

Scripture

> When he entered the temple, the chief priests and the elders of
> the people came to him as he was teaching and said, "By what
> authority are you doing these things? Who gave you this author-
> ity? - Matthew 21:23 (CSB)

Reflection

All of us have struggled with the issue of authority. Whether it be
the authority of a parent or guardian, a teacher or coach, or the long
arm of the law, since our earliest moments, we have defied authority
and sought independence in our thinking, desires, and actions.

We have even defied the authority of God. Paul personally
testifies to this when he says, "For I do not understand what I am
doing, because I do not practice what I want to do, but I do what
I hate. Now if I do what I do not want to do, I agree with the law
that it is good. So now I am no longer the one doing it, but it is
sin living in me. For I know that nothing good lives in me, that is,
in my flesh. For the desire to do what is good is with me, but there
is no ability to do it. For I do not do the good that I want to do,
but I practice the evil that I do not want to do. Now if I do what
I do not want, I am no longer the one that does it, but it is the sin
that lives in me. So I discover this law: When I want to do what
is good, evil is present with me. For in my inner self I delight in
God's law, but I see a different law in the parts of my body, waging

war against the law of my mind and taking me prisoner to the law of sin in the parts of my body. What a wretched man I am!" (Romans 7:15-24a).

On Tuesday of Holy week, the religious leaders question Jesus' authority to do what he had been doing, healing the sick and lame and preaching about the Kingdom of God. Knowing their hearts and their desire to trap and arrest him, Jesus answers indirectly. He says, "I will also ask you one question, and if you answer it for me, then I will tell you by what authority I do these things. Did John's baptism come from heaven, or was it of human origin?" (vs. 24-25). By asking this question, Jesus turns the tables and catches the religious leaders at their own game, and they know it too. They respond, "If we say, 'From heaven,' he will say to us, 'Then why didn't you believe him?' But if we say, 'Of human origin,' we're afraid of the crowd, because everyone considers John to be a prophet." So they answered Jesus, "We don't know." (vs. 26-27). In saying so, the leaders refuse to acknowledge the authority of God in John's life, and in doing so, refuse to acknowledge that Jesus might have been doing what he was doing because he was under God's authority. Jesus responds, "Neither will I tell you by what authority I do these things" (vs. 28). Of course, Jesus operated under the authority of the Father (John 5:19, 30; 12:49-50; 14:31). As a result, the Father has given Jesus authority in Heaven and on earth (Matthew 29:18).

Is Jesus the ultimate authority in your life? Are you submitting to his reign and rule in every area of your life every day? Does your struggle with sin keep you from thinking that God would want to do a work in or through you? If so, hear the encouragement from the Apostle Paul. He concludes, "Who will rescue me from this body of death? Thanks be to God through Jesus Christ our Lord!" (Romans 7:24b).

PRAYER

Father, I confess that I have challenged your authority in my life more times than I can count. Every time it leaves me wanting, realizing that anything that I substitute for you is simply a false god, and idol that doesn't satisfy. Please forgive me. I recognize today your right and authority to rule every area of my life. For you and you alone are God, and I need you to rescue me from this body of death. Please do a new work in me today and help me to consistently surrender every part of my day to you. In Jesus' name. Amen.

NOTES:

TUESDAY

SCRIPTURE

What do you think? A man had two sons. He went to the first and said, 'My son, go work in the vineyard today.' "He answered, 'I don't want to,' but later he changed his mind and went. Then the man went to the other and said the same thing. 'I will, sir,' he answered, but he didn't go. Which of the two did his father's will?" They said, "The first. Jesus said to them, "Truly I tell you, tax collectors and prostitutes are entering the kingdom of God before you. For John came to you in the way of righteousness, and you didn't believe him. Tax collectors and prostitutes did believe him; but you, when you saw it, didn't even change your minds then and believe him. - Matthew 21:28-32 (CSB)

REFLECTION

We all have choices in life. We choose daily what to wear, what to eat, where to go, and who to go there with, but sometimes we get those choices wrong. Either because of a lack of understanding our circumstances, personal preferences or biases, protecting our power or position, or simply being lazy or prideful, we can end up making poor judgments. And sometimes it is only when we suffer the consequences of those decisions or someone steps in to correct our thinking that we can see things clearly and get back on the right path.

Jesus had spoken in parables throughout his public ministry. A parable is a simple story used to illustrate a moral or spiritual lesson. His parables had caused amazement, confusion, and at times, anger among the crowds, disciples, and the religious leaders. On the final Tuesday of his life, he again enacts five parables, all during this day of teaching and controversy.

The first parable Jesus tells regards two sons, and is illustrative of God's relationship with Israel. Both sons have the same father, but respond differently to his requests. The first son refuses to go to work, but later changes his mind and did. The second readily agrees to work, but then doesn't go. The illustration is easy to understand, at least to the religious leaders. The second son is a condemnation of their willingness to serve God but failure to recognize Jesus as the Messiah. The first son is illustrative of all of those who were outcasts in Jewish society, such as the tax collectors and prostitutes, who initially refused God, but now, in light of Jesus, have believed and obeyed.

How has pride, personal preference, lack of understanding, or laziness kept you from seeing Jesus for who he is and what he wants to do in your life? What do you need to surrender to him so that he is your all in all?

PRAYER

Father, I realize that I can allow my own will to supersede yours in my life. I can get so off track, no longer sensing your presence or being able to hear your voice directing me daily. Help me to slow down, listen, surrender, abide, and obey you today. For you are my all in all. In Jesus' name. Amen.

NOTES:

Wednesday

Scripture

Then they sent some of the Pharisees and the Herodians to Jesus to trap him in his words. When they came, they said to him, "Teacher, we know you are truthful and don't care what anyone thinks, nor do you show partiality but teach the way of God truthfully. Is it lawful to pay taxes to Caesar or not? Should we pay or shouldn't we?" But knowing their hypocrisy, he said to them, "Why are you testing me? Bring me a denarius to look at." They brought a coin. "Whose image and inscription is this?" he asked them. "Caesar's," they replied. Jesus told them, "Give to Caesar the things that are Caesar's, and to God the things that are God's." And they were utterly amazed at him. - Mark 12:13-17 (CSB)

Reflection

Have you been a victim of the parent trap? Not the movie (either the 1961 or 1998 versions), but in your own home? The parent trap happens when a child (or children) goes to one parent with a problem or request, receives an answer, and then goes to the other parent separately to bring them on board with what the first parent has already agreed to, using the first parent's answer as leverage. It is a devious, coordinated, militaristic effort to divide and conquer. Unfortunately, many times, to please our children or win their affection, one or both parents might give in to their devilish schemes and give the child what they want. More astute parents will see the set-up coming and defer until they can confer with the other parent.

The Pharisees tried to do the same thing to Jesus. They sent some of their disciples and some of the Herodians, those loyal to the dynasty of Herod, who were puppet rulers under the Romans, to test, and hopefully arrest, Jesus. In an effort of false sincerity, they ask him a question about taxes. They try to play to his ego, complementing him on being straight forward in his teaching and unaffected by the opinion of others. They then ask if they should pay taxes to Caeser. The tax in question was the poll-tax, which was to be paid by all who lived in Judea. As a Galilean, Jesus was exempt from this tax, and so could conceivably speak more freely about the issue. The tax, a denarius, was equal to one day's wage for a worker. Their point was to trap him. If he said yes, then the crowd would be against him. If he said no, then he stood against Rome.

But Jesus sees through their deception and calls out their hypocrisy. In one of the most brilliant retorts in human history, Jesus calls for a coin, asks who's image it bears, recognizes it at Ceasar's, and calls them to direct their loyalty appropriately. In doing so, he reminds all of those who are listening, and us today, that loyalty to God is much more important than loyalty to any government or man, as God is over all nations and rulers. As such, we are to daily give him the priority in our lives.

Where does your loyalty lie today? We will give our lives and worship to those things that we value most, through our attention and affection. Is God the priority of your life? If not, what will need to change for him to become so?

PRAYER

Father, help me to make you the priority of my life. When other things vie for supremacy, help me to surrender them to you. Remind me that when I find myself being divided that you have called me to wholeness. Help me not to live a lukewarm life (Revelation 3:6), neither hot nor cold, but to live a life fully committed to you. Thank you. I love you! In Jesus' name. Amen.

NOTES:

THURSDAY

SCRIPTURE

And one of them, an expert in the law, asked a question to test him: "Teacher, which command in the law is the greatest?" He said to him, "Love the Lord your God with all your heart, with all your soul, and with all your mind. This is the greatest and most important command. The second is like it: Love your neighbor as yourself. All the Law and the Prophets depend on these two commands." - Matthew 22:35-40 (CSB)

REFLECTION

Write out the events of your typical weekly schedule below (you can hit the highlights or go as deep as you like):

Sunday:

_____

_____

Monday:

_____

_____

Tuesday:

_____

_____

Wednesday:

_____

_____

Thursday:

_____

_____

Friday:

_____

_____

Saturday:

_____

_____

Now, review your schedule considering Matthew 22:35-40. How does your daily life reflect love for God with all your heart, soul, mind, (and strength- Mark 12:30)? What needs to be adjusted for you to love God and others well? When you make these adjustments, you will find that "You are not far from the kingdom of God" (Mark 12:34).

PRAYER

Father, reveal to me today what adjustments I need to make in my life to love you with all my heart, soul, mind, and strength. Also, show me what I need to do to love my neighbor as myself. I want to experience your presence daily and walk in the power and purposes of your Kingdom. In Jesus' name. Amen.

NOTES:

FRIDAY

SCRIPTURE

Then Jesus spoke to the crowds and to his disciples: "The scribes and the Pharisees are seated in the chair of Moses. Therefore do whatever they tell you, and observe it. But don't do what they do, because they don't practice what they teach. They tie up heavy loads that are hard to carry and put them on people's shoulders, but they themselves aren't willing to lift a finger to move them. They do everything to be seen by others: They enlarge their phylacteries and lengthen their tassels. They love the place of honor at banquets, the front seats in the synagogues, greetings in the marketplaces, and to be called 'Rabbi' by people." - Matthew 23:1-7 (CSB)

REFLECTION

I love to go to plays, especially musicals on Broadway in New York or the West End in London. The sets, the actors/singers, the professionalism and talent displayed is next to none. In the ancient world of the Greeks and Romans, plays provided a key source of entertainment, philosophical teaching, and political pandering. Theaters were constructed throughout the Greco-Roman world to spread Greek culture and Roman rule. Some theaters, such as the grand theater at Ephesus, could hold up to 25,000 spectators. The Greek word for actor is *hypokrites* (ὑποκριτής), and means "an interpreter from underneath." It is where we get our word hypocrite. To be a hypocrite is to pretend to be something or someone you are not.

Jesus didn't have much patience for moral and religious hypocrites. In fact, on the Tuesday of Holy Week, he instructs the people to pay attention to what the Pharisees say, as the keepers and interpreters of the Old Testament Law, as long as it accords with the law, but not to do what they do because they do not live out what they teach. As a result, their teaching had become burdensome to the people, weighing them down, and the so-called experts were simply religious play actors, saying the words, but not willing to help or serve those they were over. Their goal was their own self-gratification and self-adoration.

Jesus then launches into what are called the "seven woes", or a series of condemnations against the religious hypocrites of his day. He says, "Woe to you, scribes and Pharisees, hypocrites!"... (1) "You shut the door of the kingdom of heaven in people's faces," (2) "You travel over land and sea to make one convert, and when he becomes one, you make him twice as much a child of hell as you are!," (3) [You are] "blind guides," (4) "You pay a tenth of mint, dill, and cumin, and yet you have neglected the more important matters of the law—justice, mercy, and faithfulness," (5) "You clean the outside of the cup and dish, but inside they are full of greed and self-indulgence," (6) "You are like whitewashed tombs, which appear beautiful on the outside, but inside are full of the bones of the dead and every kind of impurity," (7) "You build the tombs of the prophets and decorate the graves of the righteous, and you say, 'If we had lived in the days of our ancestors, we wouldn't have taken part with them in shedding the prophets' blood.' So you testify against yourselves that you are descendants of those who murdered the prophets. Fill up, then, the measure of your ancestors' sins!" (Matthew 23:13-32).

Where have you demonstrated hypocrisy in your walk with God or in relationship with others? In what areas of your life are you "going through the motions", but not walking in holiness and integrity? As God reveals those areas to you, will you ask him to do a new work in you so that you might faithfully walk with him and serve as an example to others?

PRAYER

Father, help me to stop play acting in the following areas of my life:

——————————— ——————————— ———————————

I confess and repent of these and ask you to do a new work in me so that I might be faithful to you and serve as an example of faithfulness to others. I want to get real with you in my faith and walk. In Jesus' name. Amen.

NOTES:

Saturday

Scripture

> While he was sitting on the Mount of Olives, the disciples approached him privately and said, "Tell us, when will these things happen? And what is the sign of your coming and of the end of the age?" - Matthew 24:3 (CSB)

Reflection

I love Christmas! It is all about Jesus' advent, or arrival. The lights, the trees, the reading of the Christmas story, the carols, and the food set the mood for the season. Hope, joy, peace, and love have come because Christ has come. But there is a second advent, or arrival that will happen. It will come at the end of all things, the *eschaton (ἔσχατον)*, when Jesus returns to take those who have placed faith in him as Savior and King will live with him forever in the new heavens and new earth (Revelation 21:1).

Tuesday of Holy Week is taken up with some of the most concentrated and longest recorded teaching we have from Jesus outside of the Sermon on the Mount. He ends his day of teaching with what is known as the Olivet Discourse, or Jesus' Eschatological Discourse, given to his disciples on the Mount of Olives outside the city walls of Jerusalem. This teaching is found in all three synoptic gospels, Matthew, Mark, and Luke, with Matthew's being the longest. His teaching centers on two specific topics, the destruction of the Temple in Jerusalem, which will happen at the hands of the Romans in 70 A.D, and the events leading up to his final return. These events are complicated, and countless books have been written on this subject.

All these teachings might be summed up by two phrases: Be ready and be faithful. He says to his disciples, "Blessed is that servant whom the master finds doing his job when he comes. Truly I tell you, he will put him in charge of all his possessions. But if that wicked servant says in his heart, 'My master is delayed,' and starts to beat his fellow servants, and eats and drinks with drunkards, that servant's master will come on a day he does not expect him and at an hour he does not know" (Matthew 24:46-50). "Therefore," he says, "be alert, because you don't know either the day or the hour" (Matthew 25:13).

Jesus *will* return one day as "King of Kings and Lord of Lords" (Revelation 19:16). The question is, Will you be ready? Another question is, What are you doing in the meantime? Are you being faithful to steward the role that he has given you in his Kingdom, faithfully serving as his witness and ambassador, and calling the nations to faith and faithfulness in Jesus? Or will you act like the wicked servant in Matthew 24, living for the world and yourself, clueless to second advent of Christ?

PRAYER

Father, make me attentive and faithful. Help me to live in daily anticipation of your second coming, but faithful to fulfill the role you have for me until then. Help me, by the power of your Holy

Spirit to accomplish the work you have set out for me and help me to encourage others to do the same. Thank you for drawing me, saving me, calling me, and commissioning me for your glory and the good of others until you come. "Amen! Come, Lord Jesus!" (Revelation 22:20).

NOTES:

WEDNESDAY OF HOLY WEEK

How happy is the one who does not walk in the advice of the wicked or stand in the pathway with sinners or sit in the company of mockers! Instead, his delight is in the Lord's instruction, and he meditates on it day and night. He is like a tree planted beside flowing streams that bears its fruit in its season, and its leaf does not wither. Whatever he does prospers. The wicked are not like this; instead, they are like chaff that the wind blows away. Therefore the wicked will not stand up in the judgment, nor sinners in the assembly of the righteous. For the Lord watches over the way of the righteous, but the way of the wicked leads to ruin.

- Psalm 1:1-6 (CSB)

Monday

Scripture

When Jesus had finished saying all these things, he told his disciples, "You know that the Passover takes place after two days, and the Son of Man will be handed over to be crucified." - Matthew 26:1-2 (CSB)

Reflection

Wednesday of Holy Week is a day of silence and contrasts. It is traditionally known as Silent Wednesday because there are few accounts of what happened that day as Jesus and his disciples retreat to Bethany to prepare for the Passover and all that will come in subsequent days. But two significant events occur on this middle day of the week, and they serve as a marker to how we and the world will respond to Jesus.

Spiritual discernment is key marker of a close walk with God. Discernment can simply mean "to judge well" or in a spiritual sense it can mean "having perception with a view to obtaining spiritual guidance and understanding." In other words, spiritual discernment is the ability to understand a situation or truth based on the facts at hand and a sensitivity to the Word of God and the leading of the Holy Spirit. The result of spiritual discernment is that a person might be prepared and act in accordance with an event yet to happen.

Jesus, of course, had incredible spiritual discernment. Following a day of intense teaching, confrontation, and controversy, he knew the end was coming. He also knew the hearts of those around him, especially those of the religious leaders. What he had known for a while was about to come to pass. In the synoptic gospels, Jesus predicted the events of this week, specifically his death and resurrection, at least three times. Matthew says, "When Jesus had finished saying all these things, he told his disciples, 'You know that the Passover takes place after two days, and the Son of Man will be handed over to be crucified'" (Matthew 16:21–23, e.g., Mark 8:31–32, and Luke 9:21–22). Though the disciples either refused to believe him, as Peter did in Matthew 16, or didn't fully understand the implications of these announcements, Jesus knew that the end had come. So, in some of the most direct language Jesus could use, he tells his disciples that in two days he will be handed over to the Jews to be crucified.

When have you had to use spiritual discernment? Has the Lord prompted something in you based on circumstances, His word, or in prayer to which you need to pay attention? What does your next step need to be? How can you be obedient to what he is leading you to do? When you are, he may use you to help change the world.

PRAYER

Father, I know that I can be clueless at times. I can get so myopic, focusing only on my personal circumstances, that I miss what you want to do in me and around me. Give me wisdom and discernment to know you and your will today. Help me to see where you are working and how I am to fit into that plan. Please keep me from being sidetracked by things that don't matter or the rumblings and threats of my enemies. Help me to walk faithfully with you regardless of the cost. In Jesus' name. Amen.

NOTES:

TUESDAY

SCRIPTURE

Then the chief priests and the elders of the people assembled in the courtyard of the high priest, who was named Caiaphas, and they conspired to arrest Jesus in a treacherous way and kill him. "Not during the festival," they said, "so there won't be rioting among the people." - Matthew 26:3-5 (CSB)

REFLECTION

I will never forget that day. A church member walked into my office and declared, "This is why I have hated you for the last seven years!" Well, won't that bless your day, week, year, and life! After the shock had worn off my face, I asked if he would like to sit down and discuss his feeling about me with me. He was glad to do just that. Over the next hour or so, my "friend" laid out his case. Honestly, it really hurt. His critique was not programmatic, theological, or even philosophical, but personal. After so many years of ministry, I can take the odd disappointment or disagreement over things, but when things turn personal, it really does hurt.

But it was in that moment that I experienced the grace of God in a way that I hadn't before. An amazing sense of calm came over me. My blood pressure dropped and my ears opened. I found myself really listening to what he was saying. A sense of compassion and even empathy swept over me as he wrapped up his argument. When the person finally ran out of steam, I sensed that I was supposed to be quiet and still. This totally threw him off, as he was bracing for the counter-offensive. In frustration, he asked, "Aren't you going to respond?" After a quick prayer, I said, "Sure." I proceed to tell the person how sorry I was that they felt this way and that if I had truly caused any of the things he was accusing me of, I wholeheartedly apologize. I counted him a brother in Christ and wouldn't want anything to come between us. When I was done, I could tell he wanted to keep the fire of his anger hot, but as he spoke, I could tell he was running out of fuel. In that moment, I was experiencing what Paul had meant when he said, "But if your enemy is hungry, feed him. If he is thirsty, give him something to drink. For in so doing you will be heaping fiery coals on his head" (Romans 12:20). Unfortunately, our talk didn't end in total reconciliation, but I felt like I had responded in a way that honored Christ.

What do you do when your enemies plot, scheme, or rail against you? How can you honor Christ, regardless of whether you are in the right or in the wrong, when they are calling for your head? Remember that Jesus, too, had enemies, and still honored his Father even while under persecution. May we imitate our Lord!

PRAYER

Father, I hate being criticized, vilified, or ostracized. It makes me feel "less than," like I don't matter, and condemned. In those times, help me remember Jesus, who "...was despised and rejected by men, a man of sorrows and acquainted with grief" (Isaiah 53:3 ESV). And help me to respond in such times as he would, with an unabashed trust in you. In Jesus' name. Amen.

NOTES:

WEDNESDAY

SCRIPTURE

> While Jesus was in Bethany at the house of Simon the leper, a woman approached him with an alabaster jar of very expensive perfume. She poured it on his head as he was reclining at the table. When the disciples saw it, they were indignant. "Why this waste?" they asked. "This might have been sold for a great deal and given to the poor." - Matthew 26:6-9 (CSB)

REFLECTION

In contrast to the plotting of the chief priests and elders, Matthew takes us out to Bethany, about two miles east of Jerusalem, where Jesus and the disciples are having a meal at the home of a man named Simon the Leper. In doing so, he introduces us to a woman who demonstrates the opposite of the religious leader's animosity, an unconditional love for Jesus. This unnamed woman (Mary in John's gospel) comes to Jesus and breaks an alabaster jar of extremely expensive perfume and pours it on his head (and his feet in John's gospel) while he is reclining at the dinner table. This incites vitriol from the disciples. They see it as a waste of resources that could have been allocated to other ministry causes, such as feeding the poor. In John's Gospel, the criticism is attributed to Judas Iscariot, who values the perfume at 300 denarii, which would equal a year's wages for a worker. John then gives us insight into Judas' motivation when he says, "He didn't say this because he cared about the poor but because he was a thief. He was in charge of the moneybag and would steal part of what was put in it" (John 12:6).

Though there is controversy regarding the timing of this anointing and who the woman is, the point is clear. Jesus loves extravagant worship. He loves it when we give with our whole heart and not out of a sense of obligation or duty. He even, at times, loves the recklessness associated with our devotion to him. He loves it when we pray with pure hearts in public before a meal. He loves it when we bless others in his name with a word or a resource. He loves it when we do what the world might consider foolishness by loving the unlovable or acting in a way that is contrary to fallen human nature. He loves it when we make much of him!

When was the last time you made much of Jesus? Have you spoken his name in public lately? Have you blessed someone by serving them in his name? Have you done something, prompted by the Holy Spirit, that seemed out of your comfort zone as well as for those around you, but understood that God was up to something bigger? What have you poured out for Jesus?

PRAYER

Father, teach me to be extravagant in my love for you. Help me to leverage my time, talents, and treasures for your glory regardless of what others think. Give me the wisdom to know when to do this publicly and when to love you by being silent or serving behind the scenes. Regardless, help me hold nothing back from you, for it is all yours anyway. In Jesus' name. Amen.

NOTES:

Thursday

Scripture

Aware of this, Jesus said to them, "Why are you bothering this woman? She has done a noble thing for me. You always have the poor with you, but you do not always have me. By pouring this perfume on my body, she has prepared me for burial. Truly I tell you, wherever this gospel is proclaimed in the whole world, what she has done will also be told in memory of her." - Matthew 26:10-13 (CSB)

Reflection

To some degree, we are all "fixers." We have spent our lives trying to fix relationships, school or work problems, personal faults, and even our own sin. But, if we are honest with ourselves, our success record is probably not very good. Though there are times when we find resolution to the problems in our lives through our own efforts, I would venture to guess we are batting about .400. Well, at least I am. That is great if you are a baseball player, but not if you are trying to navigate the onslaught of life's problems. In fact, such a record can even make you want to stop swinging. Just take your lumps and move on to the next one.

But there is a key thing you need to remember if you are a Christ-follower. Jesus is on your side! He is your unrelenting champion! He is your defender and sustainer! He is the owner of unlimited resources! As such, it is amazing how many times we don't even consult him when we are in the dregs of life's circumstances. But he is here and is ready and willing to help!

It's not surprising that the woman, Mary, did not respond to the disciple's criticism. One, they weren't speaking to her but to Jesus. Two, it was a misogynistic culture that devalued women and their opinions, much less their actions. Three, Jesus was there! Instead of her answering, Jesus answers for her. In one brief, but glorious monologue Jesus rebukes them, honors her, and points them all to something bigger. He starts by correcting the disciple's thinking regarding her actions. They were extravagant yes, but not wasteful. In fact, he calls her actions "noble." He then exposes Judas' selfishness by reminding him and the whole group that they will have ample time to minister to the poor who will always be with them. Next, he points to something bigger. The woman's actions were not just a solitary act of worship, but point illustratively to what will happen just days from now, his death and burial. Finally, he champions the woman by saying that as the good news of the Kingdom and its King are proclaimed throughout the world, her story will be a part of it (and so will theirs)! And it still is today!

Where do you need to remain silent and allow Jesus to speak on your behalf? Maybe it is with a wayward child or with an adversarial colleague. Maybe it is with someone who is persecuting you because of your faith or who is resistant to the gospel. Will you give space to the Lord of all Creation to do what he wants to do as you participate in his bigger story?

PRAYER

Father, please teach me to give you space to take up my cause. Help me to be so connected to you and dependent upon you that I will know when to be quiet and still so that you can do your work in my life. Also, help me to give you the space to work in other's lives. Help me to faithfully pray and walk in step with you so that I will know when to speak up and when to step away. Thank you for inviting me into your work and championing me. In Jesus' name. Amen.

NOTES:

FRIDAY

SCRIPTURE

Then Satan entered Judas, called Iscariot, who was numbered among the Twelve. - Luke 22:3 (CSB)

REFLECTION

Nicknames can be good or bad. They can reflect affection or derision. After living around the country, my family moved back to Texas in the middle of my 7th grade year. I loved sports, so I tried out for the basketball team and made it. At the first official practice, though, there was confusion. There were two Jims on the team. The other Jim had obviously been there longer, so the coach told us he was going to have to make up something so that he could tell us apart and he could appropriately direct his yelling! So, I became JT. It's funny, that nickname has popped up several times in my life and in certain ministry circles I am still JT. And with my friends in those circles, I like it.

Now, Judas Iscariot is a little different. Every time Judas' name is written in the four gospels, the Gospel writers always include a sidenote, a nickname if you will. They say that he is the one "who also betrayed him," "who is a traitor," or they speak of his name in the actual narrative context of betraying Jesus. How horrible it would be to forever be known as the one who betrayed Christ!

But what is going on here? Judas has been vilified, and rightly so, through the centuries, but there are other forces at work here. Luke says that Satan shows back up on the scene. We see satanic influence throughout the Gospel records through demonic possession, political oppression, and religious bigotry, but now we see his name mentioned specifically. The last time we see that in Luke's Gospel is during Jesus' temptations in the wilderness. In fact, at the end of that time, Luke says, "After the devil had finished every temptation, he departed from him for a time," or "until an opportune time" (Luke 4:13). Well, that time had now come.

It is easy for us to forget that we live in the middle of a war. Though wars constantly rage around the world among nations and people groups, all of us live in a cosmic battle of eternal proportions. It is a battle for the lives and eternity of people. We have a real enemy, Satan, the adversary and accuser, who seeks to "kill, steal, and destroy" (John 10:10). And, he will tempt us toward our own betrayal of Christ, not at the scale of Judas' betrayal, but betrayal, nonetheless. Betrayal in our words, in our integrity, in our marriages and families, and in the church. But we must remember that the war has already been won. If we are in Christ, we are already victors! Jesus has won the war over sin and death and the only thing left to be completed is the final battle at the end of time. But until then, God's grace and patience abound, giving space for as many as would receive him to come to faith in Christ. In the meantime, may we never forget that "greater is he that is in you, than he that is in the world" (1 John 4:4 KJV).

PRAYER

Father, help me to remember that I am in the middle of a spiritual battle. Help me to see every person that I meet as a fellow soldier of Christ or as a prisoner of the enemy. Help me to fight by the power of your Holy Spirit through prayer, your word, and faithfulness to your purposes in the world. Help me to recognize the enemy's activity in my life and in the lives of others and respond accordingly. Cover, protect, guard, and guide me and your church as we strive to extend your kingdom to the world. In Jesus' name. Amen.

NOTES:

Saturday

Scripture

He went away and discussed with the chief priests and temple police how he could hand him over to them. They were glad and agreed to give him silver. So he accepted the offer and started looking for a good opportunity to betray him to them when the crowd was not present. -Luke 22:4-6 (CSB)

Reflection

We all have our weak points. It might be money, cars, houses, clothes and shoes, technology, or just stuff. We see it and it glistens and glows and calls to us like Winnie the Pooh is drawn to honey. It might be power, fame, popularity, position, or prestige, and we leverage our every waking hour looking for the next rung up the proverbial ladder of success. It might be relationships, affection, or love, so we hop from one failed partner to the next looking for the utopian romance that we have always dreamed of having. In the end, they all have the same name: idol. An idol is anyone or anything that steals our affection and attention away from God.

Take a few minutes and list out some of the things that draw your affection and attention away from God. Be honest and specific. If we can't name the real cause, we might be diagnosing the wrong problem.

Now, what are you going to do about it? Will you allow the idols in your life to lead you further away from God, or will you go into spiritual rehab, allowing God to detox you from these habits and false objects of worship so that you can find the abundant life that he offers? • The course curriculum for your rehab is the Word of God, the Bible • Your classmates are the church, walking in faithful and accountable relationships with other believers • Your teacher is Christ, himself, working in you through his Holy Spirit to make you new again • Your goal is holiness and faithfulness, living out of your relationship with Christ every day • Your finish line is Heaven, so get ready for a potentially long road. But one word of encouragement. It is worth it! Oh, it is worth it!

PRAYER

Father, remind me today of how much more beautiful, loving, and satisfying you are than anything else that I might pursue. Remind me that, in the end, betraying you holds far more pain than surrendering to you ever could. I thank you that you are my all in all. In Jesus' name. Amen.

NOTES:

Thursday of Holy Week

On the first day of Unleavened Bread, when they sacrifice the Passover lamb, his disciples asked him, "Where do you want us to go and prepare the Passover so that you may eat it?"

- Mark 12:12 (CSB)

Monday

Scripture

So he sent two of his disciples and told them, "Go into the city, and a man carrying a jar of water will meet you. Follow him. Wherever he enters, tell the owner of the house, 'The Teacher says, "Where is my guest room where I may eat the Passover with my disciples?"' He will show you a large room upstairs, furnished and ready. Make the preparations for us there." So the disciples went out, entered the city, and found it just as he had told them, and they prepared the Passover. - Mark 12:13-16 (CSB)

Reflection

How do you prepare for worship? Think about yesterday. What did you do in preparation for corporate worship? Most of us woke up, maybe had some coffee or tea, ate a bite of breakfast, took a shower, picked out clothes (if you didn't do it the night before), shaved, put on make-up, and did your hair (if you have any), gathered your belongings and your family, made your way to the church, said hello to friends, deposited your family in the appropriate small group or found your seats in the worship service, and then took a breath. I know there are some variations to this list, but you get the idea. Sundays can be exhausting, and the service hasn't even begun yet.

But my question remains. How do you prepare for *worship*? Everything listed above is how we prepare to go to church. But how do you prepare for worship? What do you do to prepare yourself and your family to encounter Almighty God through song, prayer, fellowship, and study? Have you created space to connect with God before you even leave the house? Maybe it is in a formal time of preparation, like the disciples did in preparation for the Passover meal, such as a quiet time or time alone with God. You find your "chair," a place where you and God meet regularly. You get out your Bible, journal, devotional book, pen, tablet, or whatever you are using to study God's word. You still your heart and mind and ask God to meet you in that place. You commune with your Father. But maybe yesterday was more "on the fly." You are talking, silently or out loud, to God while shaving or putting on your make-up. You are praying for your spouse and kids, for the worship team and pastor (thank you!), for the Bible study leader, for the lost who will be in service today, and for the church, that we would encounter God in a powerful way and that lives will be changed. You share a verse of scripture or something God has taught you this week with your family as you drive to the church building. You challenge them to see where God is working today and to be open to what God is saying to them. And then you pull into the parking lot.

But preparation for worship is not just a Sunday/Wednesday thing. It is a life thing. We are called to a lifestyle of worship as we respond to the goodness and greatness of God in all things. So, if this is the case, how do you prepare to worship every day? Yes, in the morning, but also throughout the day, carving out specific moments to lift your praise to God, to be reminded of God's love and truth, to pray about the circumstances of the day amid the circumstances of the day, to intercede with and for others, and to give thanks at the end of the day. What will you do today to prepare for worship?

PRAYER

Father, help me to worship you today. In all that I think, desire, say, and do, help me to lift up the name of Jesus. Help me to see worship not as an event that I attend weekly, but a lifestyle that I live daily. Help me to use my home, school, work, church, community, airplane, hotel room, or vacation spot as my sanctuary this week. Help others to be drawn in to your glory as I lift up the name of Jesus. Please receive my offering of worship today. In Jesus' name. Amen.

NOTES:

Tuesday

Scripture

> When evening came, he arrived with the Twelve...As they were eating, he took bread, blessed and broke it, gave it to them, and said, "Take it; this is my body." Then he took a cup, and after giving thanks, he gave it to them, and they all drank from it. He said to them, "This is my blood of the covenant, A which is poured out for many. Truly I tell you, I will no longer drink of the fruit of the vine until that day when I drink it new in the kingdom of God." - Mark 14:12, 22-25 (CSB)

Reflection

Think about your favorite gathering associated with a meal. What comes to mind? Maybe it's family, friends, colleagues, or some other gathering of people that are meaningful to you. Or maybe it's the food. For me it is Thanksgiving dinner at my parent's house. I've always considered it the "perfect meal." So, here is how it is set up. We begin with the turkey. Traditionally, we order a Greenberg smoked turkey from Tyler, Texas (shameless plug). It's simply the best smoked turkey I've ever had. The turkey is accompanied by a light brown gravy. Beside that is the super-secret, handed down from generations, better than your mom or grandmom's dressing. It's such a guarded secret in my family that my wife wasn't blessed with the recipe until seven years into marriage (just to make sure she would stick!). Along with the main elements of the meal are a green bean casserole (not the one you are thinking of) that is beyond seconds for me, a strawberry-pretzel salad, and the oblig-atory rolls, cranberry sauce, a green fluff-type salad concoction, and some mac and cheese for my nephew. A plethora of desserts follow, including a Mahogany Cake (look it up), a coconut pie, and assorted other treats. I'm full just thinking about it. It brings such annual satisfaction and joy that I have moments during the year that I think about it and anticipate its return.

Jesus had celebrated many meals with his disciples over the three years since he had called them to follow him. He had also celebrated several Passover meals as well as the other traditional Jewish feasts with them. But this one is different. There is a sense of foreboding this time around. A sense of finality. A sense of fulfillment.

Of course, the Passover meal is the annual remembrance meal of God's dramatic rescue of the Jews from Egyptian captivity in Exodus. It was the culmination of ten plagues that God had sent on the Egyptians to convince Pharoah to let God's people go (Exodus 7-11). The final plague was the most dramatic and traumatic, as the Lord sent an angel to take the lives of the first-born children of the Egyptians. But God showed grace to his people. He told them that if they took the blood of a perfect lamb and mark their door frame, the lamb would take the place of the first born and the angel would pass over the Jews homes, sparing their lives.

God then told Moses how they were to celebrate this event in Exodus 12. The meal was to mark the beginning of a new year for the Israelites, a male lamb was taken into the home, inspected to see if it was without blemish and then sacrificed on the 14th day of Nisan (not the car) or in the first month of the Jewish calendar. The whole community of God's people were to participate in the celebration. The blood of the lamb was to be applied to the doorframe of the home, the lintel and the side posts. The Passover was to be kept forever, and God commanded Israel not to break any bones of the lamb. The Passover meal is very liturgical and symbolic. Candles, wine, salted water, unleavened bread, a green herb such as lettuce or parsley, the story of the Passover in Exodus, bitter herbs, singing, and recitations of certain psalms are all a part of the ceremony.

And this is the meal that Jesus had with his disciples on that Thursday of Holy Week. The symbolism is palpable, not only for remembering the Exodus account, but for what Jesus would endure over the next 24 hours. He chose two of the elements and related them to himself. He took the bread, broke it, and related it to his body, which would be broken so that we could be healed. He then took the wine, told them to drink, and related it to his blood that would be spilled for the remission or forgiveness of sins. As such, Jesus is, as John the Baptist had proclaimed at the beginning of Jesus' public ministry, "the Lamb of God, who takes away the sin of the world!" (John 1:29).

What do you think of when you consider the Passover meal and the Lord's Supper? What element most speaks to you of God's love and Christ's sacrifice on your behalf? What should be your response today to the body and blood of Christ, broken and poured out for you?

PRAYER

Father, thank you for being my deliverer. Thank you for the sacrifice of your Son, his body broken and blood spilled, so that we might be healed, forgiven, and live. Help me to remember today the price that was paid for all people, and help me to never take your salvation for granted. In Jesus' name. Amen.

NOTES:

WEDNESDAY

SCRIPTURE

Before the Passover Festival, Jesus knew that his hour had come to depart from this world to the Father. Having loved his own who were in the world, he loved them to the end. - John 13:1 (CSB)

REFLECTION

I love the stories of the fictional land of Narnia. C.S. Lewis, an Oxford professor and Christian apologist, who had no biological children of his own, wrote a series of children's stories in the 1950s that enlightened the imagination of kids of all ages. The stories center on the Pevensie children and their relatives who are magically transported from World War II Britian, by several different means, to the magical land of Narnia, where animals talk, trees whisper, and a lion named Aslan, the Christ figure, rules. If you have read the Chronicles, you know that Christian imagery and allegory abounds. One of the most interesting characters is a small mouse called Reepicheep. He is a warrior mouse, great in valor and mighty in character. His one goal is to serve Aslan, the King, and to one day go to Aslan's country to live forever. Reepicheep has many adventures, even at one point losing his tail, but lives to serve unconditionally and to love those he serves with his whole life. His life reflects Aslan's life, who had served him and saved him, even (spoiler alert) allowing his tail to grow back.

John's is the only Gospel that does not contain an account of Jesus taking the Passover meal with his disciples. Instead, he fills in some gaps of what happened that evening. Along with the meal, as accounted for in Matthew, Mark, and Luke, John says that Jesus got up from the supper, took off his outer garment, took a towel and tied it around himself, poured water into a basin, and began washing his disciples' feet. Peter immediately pushes back refusing to be washed, but after Jesus gently rebukes him, Peter submits to Jesus' request. Jesus then explains his actions. He says, "Do you know what I have done for you? You call me Teacher and Lord — and you are speaking rightly, since that is what I am. So if I, your Lord and Teacher, have washed your feet, you also ought to wash one another's feet. For I have given you an example, that you also should do just as I have done for you" (John 13:12-15). In other words, Jesus is calling them to imitate him, not just in the literal washing of feet, but in living out a life of service to one another and to the world. In fact, in what is known as the Upper Room Discourse (John 13:31-17:26), Jesus teaches his disciples how to live as servant leaders when he is gone. The discourse is founded on Jesus new command to "Love one another" (13:34), which is known as the Law of Christ, and ends with Jesus' high priestly prayer in the garden for his disciples and for all future believers who would come to faith because of their witness (Ch. 17).

When was the last time someone unselfishly served you? How did that make you feel? Was it surprising? Was it overwhelming? Was it awkward? How did you respond? Did you push back and refuse to be served? Did you outwardly receive but inwardly reject? Did you humbly open your hands and heart to their gift, receiving their love and generosity and allowing them to bless you? How will you fulfill Jesus' call to love and serve others as he has served you?

PRAYER

Father, help me to live and love like Jesus. Show me how to love and serve others well today. And help me to willingly receive the love and service of others today. Thank you for loving and serving me. In Jesus' name. Amen.

NOTES:

THURSDAY

SCRIPTURE

Then Jesus said to them, "All of you will fall away, because it is written: I will strike the shepherd, and the sheep will be scattered. But after I have risen, I will go ahead of you to Galilee." Peter told him, "Even if everyone falls away, I will not." "Truly I tell you," Jesus said to him, "today, this very night, before the rooster crows twice, you will deny me three times." But he kept insisting, "If I have to die with you, I will never deny you." And they all said the same thing. - Mark 14:27-31 (CSB)

REFLECTION

I have made several declarations before God in my life. Two come to mind. The first is that I would never serve as a Senior Pastor. I had been a Youth Pastor and an Executive Pastor for close to twenty years and saw all that Senior Pastors go through daily. Who would want that? Definitely not me! Then in 2011, God started to stir in me a new desire to lead and preach. I had led, preached, and taught in the church at a certain level, but I was sensing something "more." In 2012, God called me to be the Senior Pastor of a 185-year-old Southern Baptist church. A second declaration I made was that I would never follow a long-tenured pastor. I had seen the men who had become "sacrificial lambs" when they followed a 20–30-year tenured pastor and I didn't want to be put on the altar of sacrifice. And then in 2023, I received a phone call inquiring if I would prayerfully consider a different Senior Pastor position in Texas. I initially said no, but over the subsequent months, God worked in my life to call me to follow a 24-year tenured pastor. So, the lesson: Watch out in making declarations before God!

The Apostle Peter made the same type of declaration. When Jesus predicted that all his disciples would fall away once the religious leaders came for him, fulfilling prophecy, Peter declared that if even the rest of the disciples fell away, he never would. It was a bold, and even faith-filled statement. But it was also foolish. Remember who he was talking to. He was talking to Jesus. And, on top of that, this had happened before. Earlier in Jesus public ministry he and his disciples were in Caesarea Philippi in the northernmost part of Galilee. Jesus asked his disciples who people thought he was. They responded by giving several answers. He then asked who they thought he was. It was Peter who made the declaration, "You are the Messiah, the Son of the living God" (Matthew 16:16). Good job, Pete! Until he spoke again. Jesus goes on to predict his future death and resurrection. Coming off a huge win, Peter then responds, "Oh no, Lord! This will never happen to you!" (Matthew 16:22). Failure in six verses. In six verses, Peter moves from head of the class to the principal's office. Jesus responds, "Get behind me, Satan! You are a hindrance to me because you're not thinking about God's concerns but human concerns" (Matthew 16:23). Now, in the upper room, Peter repeats his mistake. Jesus responds to him by saying that even that night, before the rooster crows twice, Peter will deny him three times.

What declarations have you made before the Lord? Have they been prompted by God's will, like Peter's confession of Christ, or have they been prompted by self-centered desires that are contrary to the things of God? What was the outcome? How did you recover? What will you do next time a declaration before God is on your lips?

PRAYER

Father, help me to make declarations based on your Word and will and not on my own understanding and desires. Help me not to be a stumbling block to you or to others because I am not walking faithfully with you. Help my declarations expand your kingdom and not hinder it. And when I do speak foolishly, please correct me, forgive me, restore me, and renew me toward yourself and your purposes. In Jesus' name. Amen.

NOTES:

Friday

Scripture

After singing a hymn, they went out to the Mount of Olives... Then they came to a place named Gethsemane, and he told his disciples, "Sit here while I pray." - Mark 14:26, 32 (CSB)

Reflection

Substitute teachers, may God bless you. There may not be a more nerve-wracking, heart wrenching job than to go into someone else's classroom and carry on where the main teacher had left off. I will never forget one of my subs when I was a freshman in high school. She was an older lady, probably in her 40s or 50s at the time, which seemed ancient to us. She had a huge Texas beehive hairdo that must have stood a good half foot above the crown of her head. I can't remember if she was a good teacher or not, but do remember her back being turned to the class for most of the day as she wrote our lessons on the board. And that is where the chaos ensued. Several boys would start to break apart their wooden pencils and create games. The first was probably the most notorious and dangerous. They (not me! No, really, I didn't do this!) would gently toss pieces of those pencils and see if they could get them stuck in the sub's hair without her noticing. It was thrilling, terrifying, and entertaining all at the same time. We (all the ones who weren't playing this game, including me. Yes, including me), worked hard to control our giggles so we wouldn't give them away. That poor woman. I can't imagine what happened when she went to the bathroom to freshen up or got home that evening and brushed out her hair. Those kids were horrible! The second game was not unlike the first. They would take the tips of their broken pencils and fling them upward to get them to stick in the perforated ceiling tiles. By the end of class, the classroom ceiling looked like some modern art piece. I don't remember any of them getting caught.

I wonder if that is not how we might feel about prayer at times, not the hairdo episode, but the ceiling competition. Do your prayers feel like they are just being thrown up into the sky in the hope is that some of them might stick? Does it feel like God is distant and might have better things to do with his eternity than to pay attention to you? Does it feel like there is not a return on your investment of time in prayer because it seems like the answers are slow to come?

Jesus invited his disciples into the Garden of Gethsemane following their Passover meal together. The word Gethsemane means "oil press." It is where the olives were grown and pressed outside the city gates of Jerusalem. But it was about to turn into a place where both Jesus and his disciples were pressed into prayer. He invites Peter, James, and John a little further into the garden and invites them to remain a distance off and stay awake. The inference is that they are to be in prayer too, since Jesus is "deeply grieved to the point of death" (vs. 34). Jesus then goes off three separate times to pray. His central prayer is this: "*Abba*, Father! All things are possible for you. Take this cup away from me. Nevertheless, not what I will, but what you will" (vs. 36). Each time he returns to the trio, they are asleep. He rebukes them by speaking to Peter. He says, "Simon, are you sleeping? Couldn't you stay awake one hour? Stay awake and pray so that you won't enter into temptation. The spirit is willing, but the flesh is weak" (vs. 37), but they fall asleep two more times. In the end, he wakes them and says, "Enough! The time has come. See, the Son of Man is betrayed into the hands of sinners. Get up; let's go. See, my betrayer is near" (vs. 41-42).

When was the last time you felt the pressure and tension of prayer? What did you do? Did you dive deeper into the topic at hand, beseeching the Father on behalf of yourself or others? Or did you "fall asleep," thinking that your prayers are simply bouncing off the ceiling, leaving it to someone else to take up the slack?

PRAYER

Father, I confess to you that sometimes prayer seems like a futile effort. But your Word tells me that I am to pray, to pray fervently, to pray at all times, and to pray with many kinds of prayers and requests. Help me to be a person of deep prayer, seeking you in your sanctuary, placing praise, petitions, supplications, and requests before you, and waiting and listening patiently as you work out your perfect will in my life. Thank you for hearing and answering my prayers. In Jesus' name. Amen.

NOTES:

Saturday

Scripture

While he was still speaking, Judas, one of the Twelve, suddenly arrived. With him was a mob, with swords and clubs, from the chief priests, the scribes, and the elders. - Mark 16:43

Reflection

We all have turning points in our lives, those times that help define who we were, who we are, and who we will become. Whether it be the first time making a team, club, choir, or band, that first crush or date, graduating from high school, getting into college or finding that career we have always dreamed of, getting married, having kids and grandkids, and the list can go on. We also experience those spiritual moments that change everything. Dr. Henry Blackaby calls these "spiritual markers," those signposts in life that move us forward in our understanding and walk with Christ. It could be the first time we were invited to church, the revelation of God's purpose for our life, that discipling relationship that put our faith into hyperdrive, and especially that moment of salvation where we met Jesus for the first time. All of these play a critical role in our stories, but not all our turning points and spiritual markers are positive. We are formed not only by our victories and joys, but in our trials and defeats. The death of a parent, spouse, or child, the failure to get into your desired school or program, the loss of a beloved job, or the betrayal of a family member or a friend can deeply effect us and change our spiritual trajectory.

Jesus had experienced some "defeats" in his life. Rejection by those in his hometown. The execution of his cousin, John the Baptist, at the hands of Herod Antipas and the presumed death of his earthly father, Joseph, at some point in his life. Constant misunderstanding of his teachings and actions. Bad press. Assassination attempts. Plots to arrest and kill him. And now, betrayal at the hands of one of his closest friends.

Judas approaches Jesus after nightfall with a mob armed with swords and clubs, just in case. These are not Romans. That would come later. These are most likely Jewish Sanhedrin Guards, local police sent by the religious leaders. Judas gives the soldiers a sign; the one whom he kisses on the cheek is the one they should arrest. Of course, many in the crowd are aware of who Jesus is and what he looks like, based on his popularity during Passover week, but they wanted to make sure they got the right guy. In John's gospel, something amazing happens. John says that Jesus is the first to speak. He says, "Who is it that you're seeking?" "Jesus of Nazareth," they answered. "I am he," Jesus told them" (John 18:4-5). John then says, "When Jesus told them, "I am he," they stepped back and fell to the ground" (John 18:6). When Jesus says, "I am he," *egō eimi* in Greek, he was invoking the name of God Himself. Many scholars believe this is what is called a theophany, when God's presence and glory are manifested to people. The response of the crowd would at least indicate some kind of reaction to the Divine name or power in that moment. Jesus and his disciples could have presumably walked away, but that was not the Father's plan. Judas then steps up and kisses Jesus on the cheek, a common greeting among friends in the first century, indicating the person to be arrested. As the soldiers take hold of Jesus, Peter pulls out a sword and cuts off the ear of the High Priest's servant, Malchus. Jesus rebukes Peter's actions again, picks up the appendage, and heals the servant's ear (Luke 22:51). They arrest him, the disciples flee just as Jesus' predicted, and they bring him before the Sanhedrin, the ruling body of the Jews.

What have been the turning points in your life for good or bad? What are the spiritual markers in your life that have led you into a deeper walk with Jesus? How did these moments make you who you are today? How will they continue to form you in the future?

PRAYER

Father, when I am lonely, please remind me that you were lonely too. When I experience loss, remind me that you did as well. When I am betrayed, remind me that you were betrayed. When I am tempted to fight back, remind me that the battle belongs to you. And when I am threatened, remind me that you are *egō eimi*, the great "I am." In Jesus' name. Amen.

NOTES:

WEEK 6

FRIDAY OF HOLY WEEK

When they arrived at the place called The Skull, they crucified him there, along with the criminals, one on the right and one on the left.

- Luke 23:33 (CSB)

Monday

Scripture

Peter was following him at a distance right to the high priest's courtyard. He went in and was sitting with the servants to see the outcome...Now Peter was sitting outside in the courtyard. A servant girl approached him and said, "You were with Jesus the Galilean too." But he denied it in front of everyone: "I don't know what you're talking about." When he had gone out to the gateway, another woman saw him and told those who were there, "This man was with Jesus the Nazarene!" And again he denied it with an oath: "I don't know the man!" After a little while those standing there approached and said to Peter, "You really are one of them, since even your accent gives you away." Then he started to curse and to swear with an oath, "I don't know the man!" Immediately a rooster crowed, and Peter remembered the words Jesus had spoken, "Before the rooster crows, you will deny me three times." And he went outside and wept bitterly. - Matthew 26:58, 69-75 (CSB)

Reflection

There are few things worse than being rejected by a close friend or family member. After placing your time, affection, resources, and trust in someone close to you, for them turn around and defame, reject, or forsake you is not only heart-breaking, but infuriating. This can happen among family members, school/teammates, work colleagues, or even among church members. And broken trust is so hard to glue back together. It takes time, effort, grace, and forgiveness, sometimes spanning months, years, or generations. But with God's grace and intervention, even the most broken of relationships can find healing.

So much had happened in a span of a few hours early that Friday morning. The slow pace of Thursday evening, with the last supper and the songs and prayers in the garden, had now given way to an increased tempo following Judas' betrayal. Following Jesus' arrest, the Temple Guard took him to the high priest's house. In John's gospel, Jesus is taken first to Annas and then to Caiaphas. The Annas family were the ruling high priests in Jesus' day. Annas was high priest between 6-16 A.D, but was deposed by the Romans in favor of his son-in-law Caiaphas, who held the role from approximately 18-36 A.D. Because Annas still held powerful influence over the Jews, Jesus is first taken to him and is questioned about his teaching and his disciples (John 18:19-24). Annas then sends him to Caiaphas and the Sanhedrin, the ruling body of the Jews.

They meet illegally at Caiaphas' house in the early morning hours. By Jewish law, a capital trial could not take place during the night, so this gathering of the Sanhedrin was either an informal hearing or an illegal hearing that stretched to daybreak when sentence could be given. Regardless, we see the goings-on in the outer courtyard. Peter follows Jesus to Caiaphas' house. He is granted entry into the courtyard, probably with the help of John, who also followed Jesus and had a relationship with the high priest's house, probably through his father, Zebedee's, fishing business (John

18:15). Three times Peter is confronted, once by a servant girl, then by another woman, and finally by a small group, all claiming that he was one of Jesus' disciples. All three times Peter rejects the claim, growing in vitriol toward his accusers. After his third denial, a rooster crows and he remembers the words of Jesus in the upper room. He wept bitterly.

When was the last time you were betrayed? When was the last time you betrayed someone else? How did you respond? How did you seek to offer or receive forgiveness and rebuild trust in those relationships? What do you still need to do? What can you do today?

PRAYER

Father, it is so easy to give in to the pressure of the crowd. Please forgive me when I have denied you by not acknowledging that I am your follower, not speaking up for truth, not loving my neighbor as I love myself, or by watering down the gospel so that someone isn't "offended". You stood up for me so that I could be free. Please give me the grace and courage to stand for you so that others might be free as well. In Jesus' name. Amen.

NOTES:

TUESDAY

SCRIPTURE

The men who were holding Jesus started mocking and beating him. After blindfolding him, they kept asking, "Prophesy! Who was it that hit you?" And they were saying many other blasphemous things to him. - Luke 22:63-65 (CSB)

REFLECTION

Bullies have always been around. Since Cain did what he did to his brother out of jealousy and selfishness, bullies have always leveraged their perceived power over others to demean, devalue, and defeat. Psychologists would say such acting out is based in some latent need for identity, worth, and power, usually associated with past trauma, deep insecurity, or a lack of love. I saw this lived out in front of me in 8th grade. For some reason, probably because I was the new kid in school, I became the target of a bully. He constantly picked on me, made fun of me, and called me out in embarrassing ways, and always in front of others. One day, walking to basketball practice, I sensed his presence behind me. Let the games begin! But this time I was fed up. After a few minutes of his verbal abuse, I turned around and in no uncertain words told him to be quiet. He then grabbed me by the scruff of my collar and lifted me off the ground and against the wall. Then, with all the 8th grade vocabulary he could muster, he simply said, "Make me!" Well, knowing that I was about to die, I figured why not go for it, so I responded, "I don't make trash. I burn it!" Yes,

I know, eloquent, right? But what a way to go out. I could see it written on my headstone. But then something shifted in my enemy's eyes. It was more than anger. It was embarrassment. It was shame. It was pain. As his voice began to quiver, he yelled, "I'm not trash!" He then let go of his grip and walked away. In that moment, my enemy had become a person.

Jesus knew that his time had come. He knew that it was going to be the worst experience anyone could go through in human history. And he knew it was necessary. So, those in the Sanhedrin begin the abuse by mocking and hitting him. They blindfold him and make fun of him. They demean. They devalue. They attempt to defeat. And he took it. He would take much more. But why? Because of them. Because of you. Because of me. We are not trash. We are his beloved creation, gone wrong, but his, none-theless. And it would take the actions of bullies to bring about the redemption of the world. So, he took it. He turned the other cheek. He suffered so that we wouldn't have to suffer. And so it begins...

How do you respond to bullies? Do you push back and return insult for insult, or worse. Or do you respond with meekness (strength under control), seeing them as people in need of a Savior? When your worth and identity are tested, will you allow others to determine who you are or will you trust in the One who was insulted and suffered for you?

PRAYER

Father, I admit that there are times in my life when I feel less than, when my worth and identity are determined by the opinions and actions of others. Please remind me during those times that you suffered so that I might experience your acceptance, love, and grace. Please remind me that my identity and purpose are found in you (Galatians 2:20; Philippians 3:7-11) and not in my ever-changing feelings or in the judgement of others. Thank you for loving me so much that you will be willing to suffer so much. In Jesus' name. Amen.

NOTES:

WEDNESDAY

SCRIPTURE

Then Pilate went back into the headquarters, summoned Jesus, and said to him, "Are you the king of the Jews?" Jesus answered, "Are you asking this on your own, or have others told you about me?" "I'm not a Jew, am I?" Pilate replied. "Your own nation and the chief priests handed you over to me. What have you done?" "My kingdom is not of this world," said Jesus. "If my kingdom were of this world, my servants would fight, so that I wouldn't be handed over to the Jews. But as it is, my kingdom is not from here." "You are a king then?" Pilate asked. "You say that I'm a king," Jesus replied. "I was born for this, and I have come into the world for this: to testify to the truth. Everyone who is of the truth listens to my voice. "What is truth?" said Pilate." - John 18:33-38 (CSB)

REFLECTION

It is the question of our lifetime, isn't it? In reality, it is the question of every lifetime. Pontius Pilate, the Roman Governor of Judea, asks it in a sort of derisive way, but he does hit on something here. It is what every person throughout history is seeking to know. "What is truth?" Pilate came from a polytheistic background, from a Greco-Roman culture that believed in multiple gods. These gods were distant deities who used people for their own selfish games and ends. They were not to be loved but to be feared and appeased so as not to incur their wrath. This is evident in the plethora of Temples and religious shrines built throughout the Roman world. How religious Pilate was is unknown, but his question still spurs on feelings of discontent and disillusionment, yet with a sense of yearning.

The same feelings still exist today. The battle between relative forms of truth and any sense of an absolute truth still rages. The nomenclature of the day is "my truth," "your truth," "her truth," "their truth," etc. But can truth truly be that relative, built soley on an individual's or group's feelings or preferences? Such a form of "truth" is untenable. It might suffice in the moment, providing what we feel we need or want, but ultimately we will always run up against someone else's "truth" that is contrary to ours. What then? What is to be done? If there are two contrasting "truths," whose is correct? Does the bigger dog win? Does that make something "true?"

Jesus solves this puzzle for us. Earlier in John's gospel, he was preparing his disciples for the week of his passion and beyond. They did not comprehend the totality of what he was trying to tell them. In John 14, he tells them that they will have trouble in the world, but that they shouldn't worry. He was going ahead to prepare a place for them eternally, as well as for all who would follow them by believing in Jesus. He then tells them that they know the way to where he is going. Thomas is confused. He asks, "Lord, we don't know where you're going. How can we know the way?" (vs. 5). Jesus doesn't answer by telling him to pursue his own heart, feelings, or "truth." In fact, he turns the tables on that kind of thinking by redirecting them to something more sustainable, something absolute. So, he responds by saying, "I am the way, the truth, and the life. No one comes to the Father except through me. If you know me, you will also know my Father. From now on you do know him and have seen him" (vs. 6-7). In other words, truth isn't something manufactured by our own desires, whims, or emotions, but is something beyond us, something "other" that helps to define who we are, why we exist, and how we are to live. It is not found in a certain philosophy or religious orthodoxy. It is found in a person. And that person is Jesus of Nazareth. It is in him and him alone that truth is found because he is the truth. He is the repository of everything that was, is, and will be truth, because he is eternal. As such, he is the way to the Father, the only true God, since he is from the Father, and he is the only source to receive real and eternal life. The answer Pilate was seeking was standing right in front of him. And he is the answer we have all been looking for. He has always been.

How do you determine what is true? Is truth based on your feelings, the opinion of others, or the latest cultural trend? Or is truth something more? Is it founded on the eternal nature and word of God? What we believe will dictate how we live. What truth are you living out today?

PRAYER

Father, forgive me for seeking truth in anything or anyone but your son. Lord Jesus, I know that you are "the way, the truth, and the life." Help me to no longer attempt to orbit my life around any "truth" other than you. Be my way. Be my truth. Be my life. For that is what you are. My all in all. In Jesus' name. Amen.

NOTES:

Thursday

Scripture

They led him out to crucify him. They forced a man coming in from the country, who was passing by, to carry Jesus's cross. He was Simon of Cyrene, the father of Alexander and Rufus. - Mark 15:20b-21 (CSB)

Reflection

Following Pilate's questioning of Jesus, he presents him to the crowd as their king. With the prompting of the Jewish leaders, the crowd calls for the release of a notorious criminal named Barabbas. Pilate asks what, then, should he do with Jesus? They call for him to be crucified. Pilate is bewildered. He doesn't see the need or the justification to send Jesus to his death, but after much cajoling by the crowd, Pilate washes his hands and condemns Jesus. Jesus is then taken by the Roman Praetorian Guard, mocked, and beaten with a cat-of-nine-tails, a wicked whip-like instrument made from nine free flowing strips of leather embedded with pieces of glass, pottery, and bone meant to tear the flesh off a victim's back. He is beaten an unknown number of times, causing immense damage to his back. He was then forced to carry the horizontal post of the cross called a *patibulum*, which weighed approximately 80 to 100 pounds, up to a half a mile to the place of execution. On the way, he stumbles and falls, dropping his cross beam.

We don't know much about Simon of Cyrene, other than what is written about this moment. We know he is African, coming from Libya in North Africa, and that he and his sons were probably in Jerusalem to celebrate Passover. His sons are named, Alexander and Rufus. Some scholars believe that they are listed by name because Mark's readers knew them. But how could that be? Well, in Paul's letter to the Romans, a fellow believer in Jesus named Rufus is mentioned (16:13). If this is the same man who was a boy at the time of Jesus' death, then the mention of their names would make sense. We could also surmise that all three might have become followers of Jesus. Regardless, it was Roman practice to muster a conquered people into service whenever it was needed. Jesus had mentioned this when he challenged his disciples, "And if anyone forces you to go one mile, go with him two. Give to the one who asks you, and don't turn away from the one who wants to borrow from you" (Matthew 5:41-42). Simon was now living out this truth by bearing the cross of Jesus.

But in many ways we helped carry that cross beam as well. It was because of our sin, our rebellion against God, that moved Jesus to the cross. It was our rejection, our hatred of God's ways, that ushered him up to Golgotha. In some strange way, we all play the role of Simon of Cyrene. And because of that, Jesus was willing to die.

As Isaiah prophesied many centuries beforehand, "Surely he took up our pain and bore our suffering, yet we considered him punished by God, stricken by him, and afflicted. But he was pierced for our transgressions, he was crushed for our iniquities;

the punishment that brought us peace was on him, and by his wounds we are healed. We all, like sheep, have gone astray, each of us has turned to our own way; and the Lord has laid on him the iniquity of us all" (Isaiah 53:4-6 NIV).

Have you considered your role in Jesus' journey to the cross? Have you realized that it was your sin and rebellion, as well as that of the whole world, that was a key factor in Jesus' willingness to suffer and die? When was the last time you asked him to forgive you of your sin? When was the last time you thanked him for his sacrifice on your behalf? Today would be a good time.

PRAYER

Father, forgive me of my sin. I know that it is because of my sin, rebellion, and rejection of you that you willingly gave your only Son so that I might be forgiven of my sin and know you again. In many ways, I helped to carry that cross to Calvary. It was my sin that drove the nails into his hands and feet. It was my iniquity that was laid on the shoulders of the sinless one. It was my failure that led to his condemnation. It was my selfishness that led to his selfless sacrifice. But praise be to God! By his wounds we are healed! In the name of the One who died for me. In Jesus' name. Amen.

NOTES:

Friday

Scripture

Father, forgive them, because they do not know what they are doing. - Luke 23:34 (CSB)

Reflection

It is amazing how many words we use in a day. An 8-year study at the University of Arizona found that the average person speaks about 16,000 words a day. The study found that women spoke 16,215 words a day, while men spoke 15,669. Although women speak slightly more words than men, statistically, the difference is insignificant. One of the amazing findings is that only 5% of words people use during the day are unique words, with all others being repeated. Also, the average person uses between 2.67% and 3.35% of their vocabulary every day. That is a limited number of unique words and vocabulary that we use every day.

But in times of extreme stress and pain that we use fewer words and simpler vocabulary. We say what we feel and what we mean without a bunch of supplemental filler. We get down to the crux of the matter, or the most essential part of the issue or problem. And that is exactly what Jesus did on the cross.

Scripture records seven phrases that Jesus spoke while on the cross. These phrases are short and concise. They are contextual and intentional. They are focused and powerful. They are...

Father, forgive them, because they do not know what they are doing. - Luke 23:34

Truly I tell you, today you will be with me in paradise. - Luke 23:43

Woman, here is your son. - John 19:26

My God, my God, why have you abandoned me? - Mark 15:34

I'm thirsty. - John 19:28

It is finished. - John 19:30

Father, into your hands I entrust my spirit. - Luke 23:46

Reflect today on these last seven phrases of Christ on the cross. How do they apply to your life today? How do they show God's unconditional love for people? How do they inspire you to live more faithfully for Jesus today?

PRAYER

Father, thank you for the sacrifice of your Son. Words fail me as I consider his suffering and pain. His final words bring conviction and joy, sorrow and praise, heartache and thanksgiving. The lengths you went to give me the opportunity to be forgiven and to be brought back into a right relationship with you are staggering. Thank you, thank you, thank you. In Jesus' name. Amen.

NOTES:

SATURDAY

SCRIPTURE

There was a good and righteous man named Joseph, a member of the Sanhedrin, who had not agreed with their plan and action. He was from Arimathea, a Judean town, and was looking forward to the kingdom of God. He approached Pilate and asked for Jesus's body. Taking it down, he wrapped it in fine linen and placed it in a tomb cut into the rock, where no one had ever been placed. It was the preparation day, and the Sabbath was about to begin. The women who had come with him from Galilee followed along and observed the tomb and how his body was placed. Then they returned and prepared spices and perfumes. And they rested on the Sabbath according to the commandment. - Luke 23:50-56 (CSB)

REFLECTION

I have officiated so many funerals in my time as a pastor. Some funerals are hard, especially if the funeral in question was the result of an unexpected tragic death or the death of a child or teenager. Some funerals are easier, given the character of the person who died and their strong faith in Jesus. And some funerals are just weird or awkward, with strange music selections that don't seem to have anything to do with the service or the relative who requests to speak at the last minute and rambles on for 30-45 minutes without ever saying anything. In one of the strangest funerals I have officiated, the extended family were fighting over the inheritance. As a result, seating during the service was reserved based on which side of the fight you were on. Come on people, really?

Funerals can be weird and awkward because they remind us of our own mortality. And most of us don't know how to handle that. At the end of Friday, Jesus has uttered his last words and gave up his spirit to the Father. He was dead. For those who had followed him and were watching, such as John, Mary, and some other women, all hope seemed lost. What were they to do now?

A man named Joseph, from Arimathea, an unknown town in Judea, led the way. Three of the Gospels identify him as a member of the Sanhedrin and as a follower of Jesus. In his grief, he goes to Pilate and asks for the body of Jesus. Pilate gives permission and he arranges for Jesus' body to be taken down from the cross and buried in a new tomb that Joseph owned. Such aristocratic tombs were family tombs. A deceased person would be prepared for burial with wrappings and spices and laid on a bench in the cave-like tomb. Once the natural process of decay would take place, their remains would be placed in a box called a usury and placed on a shelf in the tomb. The bench would then be used for the next family member who died. This tomb was a new purchase and Luke says that no one had been laid to rest there yet. He tells us this for several reasons. First, so that all would know what tomb Jesus was to be buried. Second, so that on Sunday, no one would confuse his missing body with anyone else's. The women then prepare his body as best they can before sunset, the beginning of the sabbath and then leave the tomb.

What do you do when all hope seems lost? Where do you turn? In the midst of grief, loss, and suffering, will you turn to the One who has experienced them all? Will you trust the One who was laid to rest in someone else's tomb? Will you trust that the grave is not the end?

PRAYER

Father, death seems so final at a funeral service or graveside. It is a reminder of fragility and mortality. It is a reminder of how life is both cherished and wasted. It is a reminder that we are not here for long. Remind me today of the brevity of life. Help me to cherish each moment and to not waste my life on frivolous things. Help me to remember the loss that the disciples experienced on Friday of holy week. And as I do, help me to remember that, even though it seems like it, death is not the end. In Jesus' name. Amen.

NOTES:

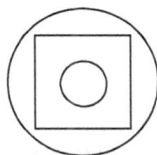

Saturday of Holy Week

The next day, which followed the preparation day, the chief priests and the Pharisees gathered before Pilate and said, "Sir, we remember that while this deceiver was still alive he said, 'After three days I will rise again.' So give orders that the tomb be made secure until the third day. Otherwise, his disciples may come, steal him, and tell the people, 'He has been raised from the dead,' and the last deception will be worse than the first." "Take guards," Pilate told them. "Go and make it as secure as you know how." They went and secured the tomb by setting a seal on the stone and placing the guards.

- Matthew 27:62-66 (CSB)

Monday

Scripture

If the Lord had not been my helper, I would soon rest in the silence of death. - Psalm 94:17 (CSB)

Reflection

There is an eerie silence around death. As a pastor, I've been in hospitals, hospices, and bedrooms when people pass away. Whether death comes suddenly, through a long battle with disease, or as the result of age, there is a sense of activity, sometimes frantic, up until the moment when the person takes their last breath. Then, there's silence. There may be a moment of intense grief, expressed in the crying, and even wailing, of the bereaved, but then there is silence. For the moment, there is nothing else to do. Hugs are exchanged. Words seem intrusive. Silence seems appropriate.

On the Saturday of Holy Week, it was silent. Jesus has died. In one final moment on the cross, he says, "Father, into your hands I entrust my spirit." Then Luke says, "Saying this, he breathed his last" (Luke 23:46). It was over. Three years of intense, life-changing ministry with promises of a Kingdom, new creation, and eternal life, now all seemingly negated on a Roman cross. Silence. Deafening silence.

But silence does not mean the absence of activity. In fact, many times it is in the silence and perceived absence of God that he is doing his greatest work. It is when we feel His absence the strongest that He is working to bring about the greatest for our life. But we must be willing to embrace the silence, allowing God to do a work in us and around us for his glory and our good.

Psalm 94 is a psalm of justice. The psalmist questions why the wicked prosper and asks God to intervene, hold them accountable, and bring justice to his people. But there is hope in the silence. God will not abandon those he loves. He will rise-up and administer justice, standing for his people and bringing comfort and joy. He is their refuge, rock, and protection even when it doesn't seem like it. But they must trust him in the silence.

Are you afraid of the silence? Are you scared of what might happen if you just stopped for a little while? What would happen if you allowed the noise of the world, social media, and your calendar to be put on hold, and you were just present with God? When was the last time you had ears to hear, eyes to see, and a heart to understand (Matthew 13:15)? Will you trust him in the silence?

PRAYER

Father, help me to trust you in the silence. When all seems lost, help me to know that you are near. Help me know that you have not abandoned or forsaken me but are working all things for my good (Romans 8:28). Help me to remember that your plan is bigger than what I can see, hear, touch, or feel. Help me to know that what you are preparing is so much greater than what I could ever ask for or imagine. I will trust in you today. In Jesus' name. Amen.

NOTES:

TUESDAY

SCRIPTURE

When it was evening on that first day of the week, the disciples were gathered together with the doors locked because they feared the Jews. - John 20:19a (CSB)

REFLECTION

Fear can be a great motivator. Fear keeps us from doing things that might put us in harm's way or put us in a position to harm others. Fear of injury keeps us from touching hot stoves, walking out in the middle of traffic, and having alligators as pets. Fear of reprisal and consequences helps us to remember the lessons of parents, grandparents, teachers, coaches, and law enforcement officers. Fear of failure helps motivate us to study, work hard, and excel. Fear can even draw us closer to God. In fact, Scripture says, "The fear of the Lord is the beginning of knowledge..." (Proverbs 1:7a).

But fear can also be a great disabler. Fear can keep us from trusting God and others. Fear can hold us back from doing things that might help us reach goals in life. Fear can keep us from developing emotionally, mentally, physically, and relationally. Fear can develop into something far worse like debilitating worry, anxiety, bitterness, foolish behavior, and significant mental or physical health issues. Fear can keep us locked in an upper room when the promise of life has been given to us.

The context of John 20:19 is the Sunday evening of Holy Week. But I think it is fair to assume that following Jesus' arrest in the Garden of Gethsemane on Thursday, when all the disciples scattered (Matthew 26:56), and his crucifixion on Friday, that the disciples most likely gathered in fear that they were next on the Jew's hit list. This fear, which was real, was also debilitating. Their Master and Lord, who had the words of life (John 6:68) was gone. Their world had grown dark. Their fear had driven them to even lock the doors, like that would be a deterrent from the authorities getting to them! But that is what fear does. It drives us to find answers that we can control instead of trusting in God. In fact, fear is a great catalyst for memory loss. Fear of the moment can make us forget the reality of God's love, presence, and promises to us. I wonder if the disciples, in their confinement, had forgotten the words of Jesus when he said, "Don't fear those who kill the body but are not able to kill the soul; rather, fear him who is able to destroy both soul and body in hell" (Matthew 10:28). Now, that doesn't mean that we shouldn't act with wisdom and discernment regarding our situation, but when we allow the situation to dictate our responses instead of God, we give fear an unhealthy foothold in our lives.

What do you fear today? What is keeping you captive in a room with the doors locked? Will you allow that fear to dominate you? Or will you remember the promises of God? Will you remember that God is not kept out by locked doors? In fact, he can walk through walls (as the disciples would soon find out – John 20:19b)!

PRAYER

Father, forgive me when I allow unhealthy fear to control me. Help me to fear (be in awe of) you more than those things that seek to dominate my life. Help me to trust in your consistent love, presence, and promises that will never fail me. And when I find myself locked in a room of my own making, walk through those walls and remind me that you are more powerful than my circumstances. In Jesus' name. Amen.

NOTES:

WEDNESDAY

SCRIPTURE

The next day, which followed the preparation day, the chief priests and the Pharisees gathered before Pilate and said, "Sir, we remember that while this deceiver was still alive he said, 'After three days I will rise again.' So give orders that the tomb be made secure until the third day. Otherwise, his disciples may come, steal him, and tell the people, 'He has been raised from the dead,' and the last deception will be worse than the first." "Take guards," Pilate told them. "Go and make it as secure as you know how." They went and secured the tomb by setting a seal on the stone and placing the guards. - Matthew 27:62-66 (CSB)

REFLECTION

We all worry. Whether it be about finances, kids, work, school, church, or a myriad of other things that vie for our attention every day, but when worry takes root, it can lead to something far worse, anxiety. And there is a difference. Worry, for the most part, resides in our minds. It is that turning over again and again of unresolved issues in our thought process that can't seem to find an end. Worry is specific, is grounded in reality, is temporary, and doesn't impair daily function. Anxiety is much more insidious. Anxiety affects both body and mind. It is more general in nature, is marked by catastrophic thinking, is longstanding, and usually impairs some kind of daily functionality.[*]

---

[*] https://www.henryford.com/blog/2020/08/the-difference-between-worry-and-anxiety.

The one text of Scripture we have that gives us insight into the Saturday of Holy Week shows us how worry can lead to anxiety. The Pharisees, the Jewish sect that were guardians of the Old Testament Law, had constantly fought with Jesus throughout his public ministry, though some like Nicodemus and Joseph of Arimathea came to believe in him as the promised Messiah. After many attempts to arrest and kill Jesus, they finally succeeded, handing him over to Pilate to carry out the final act. You would think that would be the end of it. The Jewish leaders had, along with the Romans, put down many a revolt and would-be Messiahs before. Shouldn't crucifixion have been the last word? But it seems that it wasn't. Worry, and anxiety, had beset them. They had heard Jesus say that after three days he would rise again. But really? Rise again? Was that really a threat? Probably not they thought. Though there was the story of Lazarus... No matter, the real threat was his disciples. So, they devised a conspiracy theory. His disciples will probably come and steal the body and say that he has risen from the dead. Their summary is that this "deception" would be worse than Jesus proclaiming himself as Messiah.

Pilate, probably in an effort to get all of this behind him, grants their request, places Roman guards at the tomb, and orders them to mark a Roman seal on the large stone in front of the grave. In doing so, no one would dare try to break in and steal the body. To do so would have been a violation of Roman law which brought with it serious consequences.

What is the source of your worry? Has your worry led to anxiety or worse? What means have you employed to handle it? Have you taken those worries to God? Or have you locked him up, out of the mix, sealed away, and tried to handle it on your own? Just a quick reminder. Stones are not big enough to keep him in!

PRAYER

Father, I worry about so many things. I know that you are bigger than my worries and anxieties, but I still allow them to control my thinking and actions at times. Help me when worry starts to take over. Help me when I want to keep you out of the mix and try to handle it on my own. Remind me that even when all seems dark and my hope feels buried that you are all about resurrection! In Jesus' name. Amen.

NOTES:

THURSDAY

SCRIPTURE

The eleven disciples traveled to Galilee, to the mountain where Jesus had directed them. When they saw him, they worshiped, but some doubted. - Matthew 28:16-17

REFLECTION

We have all had moments of doubt. We have doubted someone's word or promise. We have doubted someone's ability to get us to our destination or the truth of a story that seemed a little bit exaggerated. We have doubted our own ability to come through or perform when the moment called for it. We have doubted others being able to accomplish a job as well as we can. We wish we could operate more out of faith, trust, and excellence. But we doubt it!

The account of the disciples 40 days following the resurrection of Christ speaks to the issue of faith and doubt. Jesus had died, been buried, risen, and appeared to many. When they gathered in Galilee as he had directed, they worshiped their risen lord, "but some doubted," or literally "hesitated." It's amazing, but not shocking. Even in that moment, a moment of ultimate triumph and exaltation, some still questioned. Is that really him? Is this really happening? What does it all mean? What do we do now? If some of the original twelve were still hesitating regarding the events that were right before them, what were they thinking on the Saturday of Holy Week?

Doubt in its fullest form is frowned on in scripture. In fact, James says, "Now if any of you lacks wisdom, he should ask God—who gives to all generously and ungrudgingly—and it will be given to him. But let him ask in faith without doubting. For the doubter is like the surging sea, driven and tossed by the wind. That person should not expect to receive anything from the Lord, being double-minded and unstable in all his ways" (James 1:5-8). To doubt, in this sense, is to be double-minded or divided in loyalty. The disciple's doubt in Galilee following the resurrection or on Saturday of Holy Week seems to be more of a working out of the events that were unfolding in front of them. As such, doubt can become a helpful thing. Author Bill Hull says that we can see doubt as the "rebar" of our faith, helping to hold it together and make it stronger.* In other words, when we seek to grow in our faith by appropriately asking questions and seeking deeper meaning, then doubt helps to solidify what we have suspected to be true all along. In the case of Jesus' death, the disciple's doubt on Saturday (and even on Sunday morning) would lead to truths that they could not even comprehend at the time, but that would change them forever.

What questions about life, death, faith, the world, the universe, and God do you have? Write them down. Instead of allowing those questions to haunt you or cause harmful doubt, investigate them. Take out God's word and read it, listen to the promptings of the Holy Spirit, seek out wise council, read books

---

* Bill Hull, *Conversion and Discipleship: You Can't Have One Without the Other* (Zondervan, 2016), 54.

on the subjects, and let God do a work in you. I think that in the end, God will use it all to strengthen your faith.

PRAYER

Father, I admit that I have doubts at times. Even though I know you and have seen you do amazing things, I still doubt. Will you leverage my doubts to strengthen my faith. Give me the patience to trust you as I seek answers to those things that I don't understand. But first, help me to seek you, knowing that you are the repository of all knowledge and truth and that you desire for me to grow in my faith and not be double-minded and unstable in my life. In Jesus' name. Amen.

NOTES:

Friday

Scripture

"For I know the plans I have for you"—this is the Lord's declaration—"plans for your well-being, not for disaster, to give you a future and a hope." - Jeremiah 29:11 (CSB)

Reflection

When we come to moments of silence, fear, worry, or doubt, it is always good to reflect on the goodness and faithfulness of God in our lives. When we put aside the "what ifs" and begin to focus on the one "who has been" and "who is," then we get the proper perspective on our current and future circumstances.

In fact, do that right now. Spend a few minutes in reflection and prayer, asking God to remind you of his past faithfulness in your life. Once you do that, write down several specific times that the Lord brings to mind.

Now, think about your current circumstances in the context of God's past faithfulness. What correlations can you make? What steps do you need to take from here as you trust God's continued faithfulness in your life.

PRAYER

Spend some time thanking God for the things that you wrote down above. Surrender your current circumstances to him and thank him in advance for his continued faithfulness in your life.

NOTES:

SATURDAY

SCRIPTURE

Weeping may stay overnight, but there is joy in the morning. - Psalm 30:5b (CSB)

REFLECTION

So, on the Saturday of Holy Week the disciples are locked in a room somewhere in Jerusalem gripped by silence, fear, worry, and doubt. But they were also grieving. They had lost their Lord, their friend, their Master, and their teacher. The pain of grief was palpable. I'm sure there were many tears. Tears of denial. Tears of anger. Tears of confusion. Tears of shock. Tears of acceptance. They were truly lost in the labyrinth of grief.

As you think on the events of Jesus' final week, what stands out to you? The victory of the previous Sunday? The power of Monday and Tuesday? The silence and betrayal of Wednesday? The somber remembrance of Thursday? The violence and loss of Friday? The grief and confusion of Saturday?

On this final Saturday of Holy Week, take a minute and thumb back through the journey of 8 Days. Remind yourself of what God has taught you and revealed in you. How has he shaped you over this journey? How will you live differently as a result? Remember, even though Saturday reveals our deepest emotions, it doesn't compare with what is to come. In fact, because of Sunday, joy literally comes in the morning!

PRAYER

Father, thank you that even though there are tears in the night that joy comes in the morning. In Jesus' name. Amen.

NOTES:

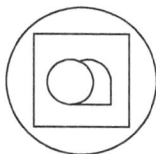

Second Sunday of Holy Week

After the Sabbath, as the first day of the week was dawning...

- Matthew 28:1a (CSB)

Monday

Scripture

Mary Magdalene and the other Mary went to view the tomb. There was a violent earthquake, because an angel of the Lord descended from heaven and approached the tomb. He rolled back the stone and was sitting on it. His appearance was like lightning, and his clothing was as white as snow. - Matthew 28:1b-3 (CSB)

Reflection

Everyone loves a good story with a happy ending. We are obsessed with the hero, especially the underdog, coming through in the end, triumphing despite overwhelming odds, and vanquishing the evil foe. Think Star Wars, Harry Potter, the Hobbit and the Lord of the Rings Trilogy, The Lion, the Witch, and the Wardrobe, and on and on...

The problem with these stories, despite how they inspire, challenge, and encourage, is that they are simply made-up stories. They aren't true. But the story of the Gospels is. The story of a loving God come to earth as a helpless baby to redeem a fallen world through the ultimate sacrifice of a Savior is true. In fact, it is the story the whole world turns on. And it is the story we are all invited to and participate in regardless of our circumstances.

The universality of this story is highlighted in the bookends of the Gospel narratives. There were two groups of people who were on the outside of Jewish society, whose testimony was not even admissible in Jewish courts of law, shepherds and women. But it was to these two groups that God chose to make knowing his coming (shepherds) and His rising (women), elevating all as recipients of his salvation.

The women, Mary Magdalene and the "other Mary" (potentially Jesus' mother along with other the women included in Luke's Gospel), came to the tomb to finish the job they had begun before the sabbath, anointing Jesus' body for proper burial. When they arrived, all was not as they expected. In Luke's Gospel, we see a conversation among them about how the stone will be moved for them to complete their mission. Matthew says that there was a divinely initiated earthquake, and the stone was rolled away by some angels, who now took up position on top of the stone. When the women arrived they saw the angels shining in their heavenly glory.

Matthew goes on to say, "The angel told the women, 'Don't be afraid, because I know you are looking for Jesus who was crucified. He is not here. For he has risen, just as he said. Come and see the place where he lay. Then go quickly and tell his disciples, 'He has risen from the dead and indeed he is going ahead of you to Galilee; you will see him there.' Listen, I have told you.'" (vs. 5-7).

They had thought the story hit its climax at the cross. They had thought the end of the story was death and burial. They had thought that there would be no sequel. Then they went to the tomb. Then they saw and heard the angels. Then they looked at where Jesus had been laid. Then they knew that this was not the end, it was just the beginning of something new! He has risen, He is alive!

When was the last time you considered the angel's words, "Don't be afraid...He is not here. For he has risen."? How does the resurrection change everything? How will it change how you live today? How will you live in his resurrection power?

PRAYER

Father, I am overwhelmed at the thought of what the women discovered that morning. To think all is lost only to find that victory has been won. Remind me today of the power of the cross and the empty grave. Remind me that this resurrection power is available to me today as I walk faithfully in you. Remind me that I don't serve a dead Savior, but a risen Lord! In Jesus' name. Amen.

NOTES:

TUESDAY

SCRIPTURE

"Take guards," Pilate told them. "Go and make it as secure as you know how." They went and secured the tomb by setting a seal on the stone and placing the guards...The guards were so shaken by fear of him that they became like dead men. - Matthew 27:65-66; 28:4 (CSB)

REFLECTION

I'll never forget being on a mission trip in São Francisco, Minas Gerais, Brazil. A joint group of Brazilian and American believers were going into this city to share the gospel through school assemblies, Vacation Bible School, street evangelism, social and medical services, visits to homes and nursing facilities, and hosting worship rallies at night for the whole city. Upon hearing of our mission, the local mayor, who was the ex-Catholic priest, banned any Catholics from coming to our services. In that city, if you joined the local catholic church, you would be given land and a home. The mayor threatened to rescind the property if any came to our services.

The spiritual warfare was palpable and we began to pray and meet to discuss what the Lord would have us do. We came to a consensus that we should go and meet with the mayor and see what could be done. The local pastor contacted the mayor's office, but he was unwilling to meet with us. But the vice-mayor was. So, we went to city hall and met with him. After an hour- long meeting, which went very well, he gave us his blessing to continue the mission in the city. Immediately we felt the spiritual oppression lift and doors began to open for the gospel. In the end, over 300 people came to faith in Christ that week!

In Proverbs 19:21, Solomon says, "Many plans are in a person's heart, but the Lord's decree will prevail." This was true in Brazil and was especially true on the Sunday morning of Holy Week. On Saturday, Pilate had given permission to the Jews to roll a stone in front of Jesus' tomb and seal it with the seal of the Roman Governor's office. He also posted Roman guards in front of the tomb to erase any doubt for the Jews concerning Jesus' death. But human plans cannot overcome God's power. On Sunday morning, angels appear at the tomb, cause an earthquake, and roll the stone away. Matthew's testimony is that the guards were so shaken that they passed out. But what happened after that?

Matthew goes on to say, "...some of the guards came into the city and reported to the chief priests everything that had happened. After the priests had assembled with the elders and agreed on a plan, they gave the soldiers a large sum of money and told them, "Say this, 'His disciples came during the night and stole him while we were sleeping.' If this reaches the governor's ears, we will deal with him and keep you out of trouble." They took the money and did as they were instructed, and this story has been spread among Jewish people to this day" (28:10-15).

In other words, the guards did not report back to their superiors or to Pilate because they would have been severely punished for leaving their post. So they went to the Jews, who concocted a plan to pay-off the guards, protect them from Roman wrath, and promote a false story that still exists to this day. But even those plans have failed as the gospel of Jesus has taken over the world. Billions of lives have been saved and changed because of his death, resurrection, and the salvation that he offers.

How do you respond when all seems hopeless, when the plans of man seem to outweigh the plans of God? What do you do when the tomb seems sealed and guarded and there seems no way forward? Will you give up and walk away or will you believe that the One who has the power over death is greater than those who guard the tomb?

PRAYER

Father, please forgive me when I think that the power of man is greater than the power of God. Regardless of the world's circumstances today, remind me that you are still on your throne, that you reign over the kingdoms of men, and that no scheme of man can outpace the power and plans of God. Thank you for being my ruling, all-powerful King today. In Jesus' name. Amen.

NOTES:

WEDNESDAY

SCRIPTURE

So, departing quickly from the tomb with fear and great joy, they ran to tell his disciples the news...Peter and the other disciple went out, heading for the tomb. The two were running together, but the other disciple outran Peter and got to the tomb first. Stooping down, he saw the linen cloths lying there, but he did not go in. Then, following him, Simon Peter also came. He entered the tomb and saw the linen cloths lying there. The wrapping that had been on his head was not lying with the linen cloths but was folded up in a separate place by itself. The other disciple, who had reached the tomb first, then also went in, saw, and believed. For they did not yet understand the Scripture that he must rise from the dead. Then the disciples returned to the place where they were staying. - Matthew 28:8; John 20:3-9 (CSB)

REFLECTION

I am a girl dad! Though my daughters are now grown, I spent my early parenting years living in the estrogen ocean. It was a world of dresses, make-up, middle school emotional trauma, and boy-friends...I was, and truly still am, a minority in a sorority! (I am so thankful for my son-in-law!). As such, I don't get boys! Though I was one, I have known plenty, and have friends that have all boys, I still don't get the destruction, noise, and stench that is associated with boys. That said, boys will be boys!

On Easter Sunday morning, Mary Magdalene and the other women do as the angel had commanded them and run to tell the disciples what they had found (Matthew, Mark, and John's account also has them encountering the risen Jesus who gives them the same instructions). When they do, the disciples don't believe them, but Peter (and John) decide to go and see for themselves and ran to the tomb (Luke 24:11-12). John then turns this into a race. He says that he and Peter run to the tomb, but that John beats him! I can just imagine Mary rolling her eyes. Boys!

What they discover, though, is life-changing! The women's words were true. It was that moment, though they didn't fully understand it all, that they believed Jesus was alive! They returned to the place where they were staying, knowing that this would change everything.

Do you believe that Jesus is risen from the dead? Do you believe that he reigns at the right hand of the Father and will one day return for those who place their faith and trust in him? Do you believe that he has equipped his followers with his authority and power to do the work he has entrusted to them? How will you live like it today?

PRAYER

Father, thank you for the power of the resurrection. Thank you that the story is true, Jesus is truly risen from the dead. Help me to live in your resurrection power today. Thank you. In Jesus' name. Amen.

NOTES:

THURSDAY

SCRIPTURE

He himself stood in their midst. He said to them, "Peace to you!" But they were startled and terrified and thought they were seeing a ghost. "Why are you troubled?" he asked them. "And why do doubts arise in your hearts? Look at my hands and my feet, that it is I myself! Touch me and see, because a ghost does not have flesh and bones as you can see I have." Having said this, he showed them his hands and feet. But while they still were amazed and in disbelief because of their joy, he asked them, "Do you have anything here to eat?" So they gave him a piece of a broiled fish, and he took it and ate in their presence. - Luke 24:36-43 (CSB)

REFLECTION

One of the hallmarks of the Christian faith is the understanding of the person and nature of Jesus. He is 100% God and 100% man. In Christian theology this is called "The hypostatic union," which was coined at The Council of Chalcedon in 451 A.D. This is the term used to describe how God the Son, Jesus Christ, took on a human nature, yet remained fully God at the same time. Jesus always had been God (John 1:1-5; 8:58; 10:30), but at the incarnation Jesus became a human being (John 1:14). The addition of the human nature to the divine nature is Jesus, the God-man. He is one Person, fully God and fully man, and his two natures, human and divine, are inseparable forever. As a result, his humanity and divinity are not mixed but are united without loss of separate identity.

We see this mystery, and it is a mystery, on that Sunday evening of Holy Week. Miraculously, Jesus appears before the disciples in the place where they were staying. In John 20:19, John says that they were hiding with the doors locked in fear of the Jews. But locked doors, just like sealed tombs, can't keep Jesus out! So he appears to them and it freaks them out. They were stricken with panic because they thought they were seeing a ghost or spirit. But Jesus quickly assuages their fear with several proofs. He points out his hands and feet and offers for them to touch him. He then asks for something to eat, though he didn't need it, and ate a piece of fish in their presence.

The emotion was overwhelming. Fear. Confusion. Comprehension. Joy. All at the same time. This Jesus was not just a good teacher and rabbi. He was not just the promised Messiah. He was not just a friend and confidant. He was truly God in the flesh, Immanuel, God with us. And he was with them, walking through walls and eating fish. The God-man. And he is with us. Now sitting at the right hand of the Father, but giving us his Spirit, who indwells every believer, communing and daily proving his reality in our lives.

When was the last time you sensed Jesus' presence in your life? How did you respond? Were you fearful? Were you confused? Were you overwhelmed? Were you joyful? The Christian faith is all about a relationship with a risen King, King Jesus. How, when, and where will you meet with him today?

PRAYER

Father, help me to recognize your presence today. Help me to know that you desire to have a relationship with me and me with you. Help me to slow down enough to sense you, listen to you, and talk with you. Help me then to do what you ask of me. Thank you for loving me that much. In Jesus' name. Amen.

NOTES:

FRIDAY

SCRIPTURE

After this, Jesus revealed himself again to his disciples by the Sea of Tiberias. He revealed himself in this way: Simon Peter, Thomas (called "Twin"), Nathanael from Cana of Galilee, Zebedee's sons, and two others of his disciples were together. "I'm going fishing," Simon Peter said to them. "We're coming with you," they told him. They went out and got into the boat, but that night they caught nothing. When daybreak came, Jesus stood on the shore, but the disciples did not know it was Jesus.
- John 21:1-4 (CSB)

REFLECTION

I've heard it so many times over the course of 30+ years of ministry. It has come from teenagers, college students, and adults. It is the main apologetic for a life not committed to following Jesus. It holds great weight, at least in the mind of the one saying it. It always acts as an attempt to close the door on a conversation about God, Jesus, and salvation. It is a mighty weapon that keeps us from being all that God desires us to be. What is this all-encompassing treatise? "But you don't know what I've done. God would never forgive me!"

It is said with such power, such vitriol, such finality, and such shame. It seems like a dead-end road, with no way out. Stuck. Lost. With no hope. Left for dead. And from a non-believer's standpoint, they are right. Paul says, "And you were dead in your trespasses and sins in which you previously walked according to the ways of this world, according to the ruler of the power of the air, the spirit now working in the disobedient. We too all previously lived among them in our fleshly desires, carrying out the inclinations of our flesh and thoughts, and we were by nature children under wrath as the others were also" (Ephesians 2:1-3).

And then there is verse 4. Paul says, "But God..." You see, for those who propose this apologetic, they forget a few things (or maybe they don't know). First, they forget Peter. Remember Thursday night? What a horrible night. Three times Peter denies Jesus before the rooster crows, and he locks eyes with Jesus (Luke 22:61). If anyone had an excuse to say, "But you don't know what I've done. God would never forgive me!," it would be Peter. But he also knew Jesus. He knew the saving power that he had witnessed for three years. Was there any hope? Could he be forgiven? He had now seen the risen Lord, but Jesus had not brought up his indiscretion, until now.

Peter and the other disciples do what they knew to do after the resurrection. They went fishing. The risen Jesus appears on the shore and asks if they had caught any fish. They respond by saying no and he instructs them to cast the net over the right side of the boat and they will find a catch (sound familiar?). They do and they catch more than they can carry. John then realizes that it is Jesus and Peter jumps overboard. John won't beat him to Jesus this time! The rest of the disciples get to shore, and they all have breakfast with Jesus (vs. 5-14).

Jesus then takes Peter aside and has the conversation that Peter was dreading. But instead of condemnation, Jesus asks three times if Peter loves him. All three times Peter says that he does. Each time, Jesus instructs him to "feed my lambs" or "shepherd my sheep" (vs. 15-17). In one glorious conversation, the events of Thursday are erased and a new and forgiven future is born. Jesus then predicts the way that Peter would die and reissues the same command he had first given Peter on the shores of the Sea of Galilee, "Follow me" (vs. 18-19).

Second, they forget the overwhelming grace and mercy of God. Paul continues his proclamation, "But God, who is rich in mercy, because of his great love that he had for us, made us alive with Christ even though we were dead in trespasses. You are saved by grace! He also raised us up with him and seated us with him in the heavens in Christ Jesus, so that in the coming ages he might display the immeasurable riches of his grace through his kindness to us in Christ Jesus. For you are saved by grace through faith, and this is not from yourselves; it is God's gift— not from works, so that no one can boast. For we are his workmanship, created in Christ Jesus for good works, which God prepared ahead of time for us to do" (Ephesians 2:4-10).

What have you done that you think is too much for God to forgive. How far do you feel like you have fallen from his grace and mercy? There is an answer to the dead-end street. Turn around! Jesus is waiting for you to have a walk on a beach. He is waiting to restore you, forgive you, and commission you. If you will just turn around.

PRAYER

Father, thank you for your unending grace and mercy. I don't deserve it! I don't deserve you! But I know that you love me so much that you are willing to forgive me. You forgive my slightest to my greatest transgression. Please forgive me today. I confess and repent (turn around) of my sin and ask you to please give me a new beginning. Help me to follow you. Thank you for your love and forgiveness. In Jesus' name. Amen.

NOTES:

SATURDAY

SCRIPTURE

The eleven disciples traveled to Galilee, to the mountain where Jesus had directed them. When they saw him, they worshiped, but some doubted. Jesus came near and said to them, "All authority has been given to me in heaven and on earth. Go, therefore, and make disciples of all nations, baptizing them in the name of the Father and of the Son and of the Holy Spirit, teaching them to observe everything I have commanded you. And remember, I am with you always, to the end of the age." - Matthew 28:18-20 (CSB)

REFLECTION

We all desire purpose in life. In fact, the Mayo Clinic cites that "those with a purpose live longer, sleep better and have a more robust immune system, lower stress levels and better cognitive function."[*] Conversely, according to a recent survey from the Harvard Graduate School of Education, "A lack of purpose or direction in life may be an important contributing factor to high levels of mental health concerns among young adults."[**] We all need purpose and meaning in life, feeling like we contribute not only to our own health and benefit, but to that of others.

---

[*]   https://www.mayoclinichealthsystem.org/hometown-health/speaking-of-health/purpose-and-mental-health.

[**]   https://www.psychiatry.org/news-room/apa-blogs/purpose-in-life-less-stress-better-mental-health#:~:text= A%20lack% 20of%20purpose% 20or,they%20could%20 compound%20each%20other.

Forty days after Jesus' resurrection, he meets with his disciples in Galilee. His purpose is to give them his final instructions before ascending to the right hand of the Father. In essence, he is handing over his mission of new creation and reconciliation to his closest followers to live out in the world. In doing so, he gives them and all believers who follow them a new vocation. Most of us work our whole lives toward a vocation. We go to school, receive technical training, or enter the military so that we might be equipped to do a job and earn a living. But the vocation Jesus is talking about in Matthew 28 (and in Mark 16, Luke 24, John 20, and Acts 1) is what we might call our "super-vocation," one that supersedes everything else we do and is eternal in nature. Once we understand our "super-vocation," we can put our earthly vocation in proper perspective. Our daily vocation, then, simply becomes the context for living out our "super-vocation."

So, what is this "super-vocation?" We are to make disciples who make disciples. In other words, as we grow to maturity in our relationship with Jesus, we are to help others to do the same. That begins with sharing the gospel with others, but it doesn't end there. Once someone comes to know Christ, it is our responsibility to help them to grow with Jesus toward Christ-likeness. In other words, our super-vocation is leading every generation toward a fully-formed life with Jesus.

So, how do we do this? Jesus tells us. We are to baptize people in the triune name of the Father, Son, and Holy Spirit. In other words, after sharing the gospel with someone and them coming to faith in Christ, we are to help them make that decision public through believer's baptism. This ordinance of the church helps them to take the first step in "gospeling" themselves as they make a declaration of their allegiance to King Jesus. Secondly, we are to help them understand and apply everything Jesus taught us. This is a lifetime endeavor as the believer is being formed, by the power of the Holy Spirit and their relationship with other believers, to desire, think, and act more like Jesus. And you and I have been invited into this process. We are to be disciple-makers. Paul put it like this: "Therefore, we are ambassadors for Christ, since God is making his appeal through us. We plead on Christ's behalf, "Be reconciled to God" (2 Corinthians 5:20).

What is your vocation? Maybe right now you are a student, in the military, in between jobs, in the middle of a career, or retired. Regardless, how are you living out your "super-vocation" in the context in which God has placed you? How are you serving as Christ's ambassador to those around you, helping them to discover him and grow to maturity in a relationship with him. For that truly is your vocation and his commission on your life.

PRAYER

Father, help me to see the bigger picture of your Great Commission and how it applies to my life. Help me to know how you have invited me into your work of new creation in the world. Help me to be obedient to grow in Christlikeness and help others to do the same. I surrender my all to you and your will for my life. Help me to follow you and make disciples who make disciples. In Jesus' name. Amen.

NOTES: